ARCTIC REFUGE

THE ARCTIC REFUGE

Tamayariak River

Shublik Mountains

Elupak

Kuluruak

Red Sheep Creek

Guilbeau Pass

Coleen River

Canning River

Sheenjek River

Table Mountain

Kuirzinjik Lake

Firth River

Old Woman Creek

Old Man Creek

Bear Mountain

Yankee Ridge

Old Crow River

Joe Creek

Demarcation Bay

Icy Reef

Siku Lagoon

Egaksrak River

Kongakut River

Aichilik River

Whale Mountain

Bathtub Ridge

Nuvagapak Lagoon

Barter Island

Jago River

Hulahula River

Okpilak Lake

Ramanzof Mountains

Manning Point

Mt. Chamberlain

Leffingwell Fork

Mt. Isto

Okerokovik River

Okpirourak Creek

Camden Bay

Sadlerochit Mountains

Nelsaluk Pass

John River

Pokok Lagoon

Tamayariak River

Lake Schrader

Double Moutain

Drain Creek

Lake Peters

Kogotpak River

Niguanak River

Plug Mountain

Mt. Greenough

Caribou Pass

Arey Lagoon

Kaktovik

Ambresvajun Lake

Esetuk Creek

Kolotuk Creek

East Patuk Creek

West Patuk Creek

ARCTIC REFUGE
A CIRCLE OF TESTIMONY

Compiled by
Hank Lentfer and Carolyn Servid

CONTENTS

"We hurt because we see the land being destroyed. We believe in the wild earth because it's the religion we're born with. After 10,000 years our land is still clean and pure. We believe we have something to teach the world about living a simpler life, about sharing, about protecting the land."

—TRIMBLE GILBERT, CHIEF OF ARCTIC VILLAGE

A CALL TO GATHER

It started with a phone call, an evening sometime in mid-January.

The land between our homes is cut and dippled by the countless fjords and islands of southeast Alaska. It takes five days of decent weather to make the trip by sailboat, twice that in a kayak. With the steady winter winds buffeting the trees and stirring up waves, we were both far too cozy to travel. We settled for the immediacy and convenience of the phone.

We had not seen each other since summer, had not talked since the election of our new president. Our voices, carried through winter's dark by the mystery of satellites, conveyed a common heaviness. Daily, the news revealed what we already feared. We knew it was coming, but we still marveled at the swiftness and intensity of the efforts to open public lands to the insatiable appetite of industry. We felt baffled by the blatant disregard for the environment. We worried for the well-being of the planet itself. There is a deep loneliness in the face of such news. Yet, from such loneliness grows the power, the necessity of community.

We hung up the phone feeling hopeful. The new administration was focused on opening the Arctic National

Wildlife Refuge to oil drilling. We would start there. We would amplify the voices in favor of conservation by inviting writers to contribute to an anthology in support of the Refuge. We would send the collective words to Congress, to the president, to anyone who would listen. Within a week we had drafted a letter and sent it to over fifty writers around the country. Everybody we talked to knew of someone else who was passionate about the Refuge. Word spread, the original letter was copied and sent on. Private donations were made to cover the cost of printing. A photographer graciously donated his work. A Sitka artist put her other projects aside and spent five preciously sunny days indoors creating the drawings. Authors rearranged their calendars to travel to D.C. for a press conference and lobbying effort. More donations came to cover travel expenses.

A quick month after our phone call, the writings rolled in. Two or three a day. More donations of words, time, and heart than we could put in a single volume. The authors, from global leaders to nomadic hunters, offer perspectives as diverse as the places they call home, from Arctic Village to Port Royal, Kentucky. They speak with the training of scientists and the passion of poets. Their words concern global warming and the need for a sustainable energy policy. They worry about hibernating polar bears and migrating caribou. They offer lessons from indigenous cultures and stories about the healing properties of open space.

They speak of a richness outside of bank accounts, stock portfolios, and new homes. A richness felt in the midst of a sea of migrating caribou, bodies wavering from horizon to horizon. A richness enhanced by rarity. A richness that echoes a rhythm far older than the rise of our young nation. A richness that once spent, like buffalo and tallgrass prairie, will not return.

These writers draw from their diverse backgrounds and paint a painful picture of what will drain from our lives if the oil companies are allowed to build another industrial complex across yet another piece of the Arctic. They weave together a compelling story of the folly and danger of human greed and the wisdom of restraint. They draw a circle of testimony centered on the hope of an undeveloped refuge in the Arctic.

When a lone wolf howls it sounds distinctively alone. When a pack howls, the sounds harmonize and mix until the voices of a few blend into the chorus of a multitude. A call answered and passed on. A call to gather. Such are the writings you hold in your hand.

HANK LENTFER
(B. 1966)

CAROLYN SERVID
(B. 1953)

ARCTIC REFUGE

WE ARE THE ONES WHO HAVE EVERYTHING TO LOSE

Maybe there are too few of us to matter. Maybe people think Indians are not important enough to consider in making their energy decisions. But it's my people who are threatened by this development. We are the ones who have everything to lose.

We are the caribou people. Caribou are not just what we eat; they are who we are. They are in our stories and songs and the whole way we see the world. Caribou are our life. Without caribou we wouldn't exist.

From the time I was very young, I remember my father going out hunting. He had a trapline up on the Salmon River, a hundred miles from his nearest neighbor. I had seven brothers and sisters and we had to work to survive. I helped with chores every day. I cut wood, snared rabbits, fished for grayling. Sometimes I'd go beaver snaring with my father, to help him and to learn the way. I never went to school until I was thirteen, but I learned from living out in the wilderness, our natural world. It's a good life—fishing, hunting, gathering berries and roots.

We never got bored. In fall we had ice skating and fishing. In winter we played in snow drifts. And in the evenings my older brother, Gideon—he's chief at Venetie now—would read to us. My dad would make snowshoes and toboggans and harnesses—everything that we used. And we would help with that. Our mom—everything that we wore, she sewed. And she did the tanning, fur sewing, and beadwork.

In June of 1988, our Gwich'in elders got concerned about the oil companies wanting to go drill where the caribou have their calves. So they called a meeting in Arctic Village. People came in from all our villages. Some paid to bring their whole families. Our chiefs went up into the hills and around a campfire they made a pact to protect the birthplace of the Porcupine Caribou Herd and our Gwich'in way of life.

We learned a lot from that Exxon *Valdez* oil spill. We've still got clean air and water and we want to keep it that way. There are places that shouldn't be disturbed for anything. Some places are too important, made especially for the animals. The calving grounds must be left alone.

We've heard Roger Herrera from British Petroleum say that "It's inevitable that these Gwich'in people will have to change." But we don't want to change our way of life. We have been here for thousands of years. We know the weather, the animals, the vegetation, and the seasons. We are capable of living up here if others would only respect our ways and our judgment.

The oil companies keep saying that all their roads and pipelines aren't going to bother the caribou. But we know the caribou. We know they don't like all that stuff, especially when they are having their calves. We are concerned about all the salt and chemicals they put on their roads. It can drain onto the tundra, get into the water, and be unhealthy for the young caribou. A report from the Canadian government tells us that the caribou have already been disturbed around the oil fields. If we lose the caribou there will be no more forever.

But our fight is not just for the caribou. It's for the whole ecosystem of Gwich'in country, which covers northeast Alaska, the northern part of the Yukon Territory, and the McKenzie Delta. And our fight is a human rights struggle—a struggle for our rights to be Gwich'in, to be who we are, a part of this land.

The coastal plain itself is a birthing place for so many creatures that we call it "Where Life Begins." Fish come here from the Arctic Ocean to spawn. Polar bears den along the coast. Wolves and grizzlies and wolverines have their young here. And many kinds of birds from different parts of the world come here to nest.

We have proposed a biocultural preserve to protect the land and Native people, and the wild creatures on both sides of the Alaskan-Canadian border. We've also asked for wilderness status in the Refuge because that looks like the best way to protect our culture from all this industrial pressure.

We know the oil companies will come at us again. More battles lie ahead. We have to protect the caribou. It will be hard. We have to work together. The Gwich'in are going to fight as long as we need to. We know that without the land and the caribou we are nobody.

SARAH JAMES
(B. 1944)

A PRESIDENTIAL PERSPECTIVE

Rosalynn and I always look for opportunities to visit parks and wildlife areas in our travels. But nothing matches the spectacle of wildlife we found on the coastal plain of America's Arctic National Wildlife Refuge in Alaska. To the north lay the Arctic Ocean; to the south, rolling foothills rose toward the glaciated peaks of the Brooks Range. At our feet was a mat of low tundra plant life, bursting with new growth, perched atop the permafrost.

As we watched, 80,000 caribou surged across the vast expanse around us. Called by instinct older than history, this Porcupine (River) Caribou Herd was in the midst of its annual migration. To witness this vast sea of caribou in an uncorrupted wilderness home, and the wolves, ptarmigan, grizzlies, polar bears, musk oxen, and millions of migratory birds, was a profoundly humbling experience. We were reminded of our human dependence on the natural world.

Sadly, we also were forced to imagine what we might see if the caribou were replaced by smoke-belching oil rigs, highways, and a pipeline that would destroy forever the plain's delicate and precious ecosystem.

Unfortunately, that scenario is far from imaginary. The reason the Alaskan coastal plain is home today to a pageant of wildlife is that there have been both Republican and Democratic presidents who cared about the environment. In 1960 President Dwight D. Eisenhower designated the coastal plain as part of a national wildlife refuge. Twenty years later, I signed legislation expanding the protected area to 18 million acres. I listened to scientists who emphasized that the coastal plain is the ecological heart and soul of this, our greatest wildlife sanctuary. And I decided we should do everything possible to protect it and the stunning wildlife that it shelters. At my urging, the House twice voted to dedicate the coastal plain as statutorily protected wilderness.

Then, even more than today, much attention was focused on high energy prices; oil companies playing on Americans' fears sought the right to drill in protected areas. While the House held firm, the Senate forced a compromise, without ever putting the fate of the Refuge to a vote. Thus, the law I signed twenty years ago did not permanently protect this Arctic wilderness. It did, however, block any oil company drilling until Congress votes otherwise. That is where the issue stands today.

The fate of the Arctic coastal plain was a subject of intense debate in the presidential campaign. But as the 106th Congress adjourned, a bill to safeguard the coastal plain by designating it as wilderness was blocked by parochial opposition from Alaska's congressional delegation. President George W. Bush and Vice President Dick Cheney have wasted no time in pressing Congress to open this area to oil companies. As oil industry veterans, they have what I believe is misguided faith that drilling would have little impact.

The simple fact is, drilling is inherently incompatible with wilderness. The roar alone of road building, drilling, trucks, and generators would pollute the wild music of the Arctic and be as out of place there as it would be in the heart of Yellowstone or the Grand Canyon.

Some 95 percent of Alaska's oil-rich North Slope lands already are available for exploration or development. Our nation must choose what to do with the last 5 percent. Oil drilling or wilderness. We cannot have it both ways.

I am for the wilderness. That is why I urge all members of Congress to stand in opposition to drilling in the refuge. Never before has the Arctic been so threatened. Never before has there been such a dire need for a strong, unwavering voice in support of wilderness.

When Teddy Roosevelt used the Antiquities Act to protect the Grand Canyon, he said: "Leave it as it is. The ages have been at work on it, and man can only mar it. All you can do is keep it for your children, your children's children, and for all who come after you."

That same foresight is needed now. The fate of the Arctic National Wildlife Refuge is in your hands. I urge you all to look beyond the benefits of short-term economic gain to the gift you are able to leave for our grandchildren.

JIMMY CARTER
(B. 1924)

A CONGRESSIONAL PERSPECTIVE

During my sixteen years in Congress, it was my good fortune to chair the subcommittee responsible, on the House side, for processing legislation to shape the future of the American people's land in Alaska. The Alaska Lands Act of 1980 (ANILCA) was the ultimate result of our work. This involved many weeks of traveling all over Alaska, listening to the people, marveling at the wildlife, and being thrilled by the awesome natural beauty of the Great Land.

After my first visit to Alaska, I summarized the challenge as follows:

> Will the spectacular scenery bear the scars of mining and clear-cutting and the clutter of commercial development? Will the tundra be marred by vehicle tracks? Will the rivers, lakes, and beaches be polluted and the wildlife depleted or squeezed into a few small preserves? Will the native culture be atrophied as a result of the destruction of its ecological base? All this could happen quite easily. Indeed, because the natural ecology of the Arctic is far more fragile than that of temperate zones, it will happen, unless "development" is carefully controlled and, in some places, prohibited entirely.

I believe that Congress, in passing ANILCA, successfully met the challenge and appropriately resolved most of the conflicts between resource exploitation and preserving Alaska's wilderness values. Thus, despite huge pressure from the oil industry, the Act prohibits oil development on all federal land in the coastal plain of the Arctic National Wildlife Refuge. But today new voices are clamoring for opening that magnificent wilderness to oil exploration and development. This, despite the fact that government studies indicate that it would produce little oil for the next ten years and then but 1 or 2 percent of the nation's oil consumption.

The sad fact is that oil development in ANWR would be devastating to its marvelous wildlife and would permanently destroy the wilderness character of that fragile area. If anyone doubts it, they need only visit the Prudhoe Bay oil field. Beyond that, deciding whether to develop ANWR brings us face to face with a moral issue, which was perhaps best stated by one of the native Alaskan elders at our hearing in the fishing village of Togiak in 1977. "If we destroy the land," he said, "God, in his mercy, will forgive us, but our children won't."

John F. Seiberling

JOHN SEIBERLING
(B. 1918)

TEA WITH MARDY

We sit by the fire surrounded by shelves of natural history books. With white hair framing her face, Mardy Murie's cheeks are still rosy, perhaps because of all the years spent exploring the wilderness. At ninety-eight years, her speech has slowed, but her eyes are a window to the heart. She continues to love life and the natural world around her rustic log home in Moose, Wyoming.

While we sip our tea, snowflakes drift through the sky and chickadees flit by the feeder. We share stories about her beloved Arctic Refuge, the extraordinary place that we both cherish. With great passion and tireless devotion, she and her husband, Olaus, worked to establish the original Arctic Wildlife Range. Without their vision and leadership in the 1950s, America's northernmost refuge may have never graced the map.

Mardy asks me to recount my experience of being surrounded by caribou on the coastal plain of the Arctic Refuge. I hold her warm hand, and she listens intently.

On that July day, I stood on the coastal plain along the Egaksrak River. The majestic Brooks Range loomed behind me, pressing the open tundra toward the ice-mantled Arctic Ocean. The rush of river, lilting song of the Lapland longspurs, and whine of mosquitoes filled the air. I watched a buff-colored sandpiper chick wobble through the grasses, snatching mosquitoes. It seemed a miracle that such a tiny fluff of life would later migrate thousands of miles to places like the coast of Venezuela.

Looking east beyond the flower-specked tundra, the entire horizon wavered. At first I thought it was only a mirage, but soon realized it was not imaginary figures bubbling up from the tundra. Caribou by the tens of thousands were approaching. Shoulder to shoulder, they streamed across the tundra, a tide of flesh and blood. Within a few minutes, the endless procession of animals flooded the tundra before me. There was barely a trace of ground through the mass and clutter of hooves.

Immersed within the herd, a steady chant of grunts, bleats, and clicking hooves created a caribou symphony. I was close enough to hear calves pant from the heat and caribou teeth clip the tundra plants. Gradually the swarm of animals ebbed away from the river. Their voices grew muffled, then faint. Their bodies became distant silhouettes against the white, sparkling sea ice. It was life in the Arctic, at its fullest moment of creation, in the wildest of landscapes.

Snowflakes still lace the sky, and Mardy studies them while she listens.

"I worry about the Arctic. What do you think will happen?" she asks.

I explain that I'm optimistic, that many members of Congress want to protect the area, and the conservation fight is stronger than ever. More and more Americans are learning about the Arctic and working to permanently protect it from oil development.

"We will win this fight," I say, in an effort to ease her mind.

"I need some kind of assurance," she replies.

"It's a promise. We will win and keep it wild."

I kiss her on the forehead and thank her for all her work to save the Arctic. She is an inspiration. Tears welling, I say good-bye and walk out the door.

"Go out and enjoy it all," she says enthusiastically.

Walking out into a flurry of snow, I see her wave good-bye through the window. I ponder over Mardy's love for the Arctic, and her passion to protect the area. We must win, I think. We *must* win.

For Mardy. For the wandering caribou and birds. For our children. And for the precious wilderness itself.

DEBBIE MILLER

(B. 1951)

LETTER TO THE PRESIDENT

Dear Mr. President,

I care very deeply about the fate of the Arctic National Wildlife Refuge. I want to do whatever I can to help protect it. I feel like I cannot do enough, and I have such tenderness for the precious place. As a people, we feel protected by you. You can do what needs to be done to save this area. I stand by the man who can do the most to protect it.

A treasure like the Refuge can only be protected by people who are sensitive enough to do just that. I believe this place means something to every citizen. This is a very great gift you can give to the people. It is good to give consideration to people who care so strongly about something.

I hope you can visit the refuge so you will understand me even better.

My regards,

Margaret E. Murie

MARDY MURIE
(B. 1902)

TURNING

I first came here to the Arctic National Wildlife Refuge to kill. I was a hard youth, full of blood lust. We landed on a gravel bar of a river, I can't recall its name if it even had a name. But I recall the feel of landing, how the plane rattled in fast, and we debarked, and I looked around and felt the full expanse of this place for the first time. It was an instant recognition. I felt my life just beginning, and I knew that I would always want more of it, of this kind of space and primordial wild. It was called the Arctic Wildlife Range then, a relatively new designation, unknown to all but a few. I never imagined it could be threatened. I was twenty-five years old that first time coming here. Thirty-one years ago. How my life has turned in that time, my heart opened and softened.

But enough of that. Stand here at the edge of the Arctic Ocean with me and look north. Look out toward the far end of nothing, the seemingly endless white expanse that circles the northern reaches of our globe, out there where great white bears hunt ringed seals and the world turns on its axis. Only a very few have ventured much beyond where we stand.

Look down now. Narrow, gray gravel beach. Feel it

beneath your boots. These stones are hundreds of millions of years old, here long, long before the planet had any notion of our slow, hairless, upright species. Perhaps, during the Pleistocene when this was all a rich grassland, woolly mammoths and saber-toothed cats and giant ground sloths trod upon these very stones. Even before that, before the evolution of mammals, during the Carboniferous period, this place was tropical and lush, covered with a rich tangle of plants. For several million years the plants collected sunlight and photosynthesized and thrived and died and accumulated mass. Ancient sunlight, buried and compressed into a thick black sludge now far beneath our feet. Yes, it's most likely down there, holding us. We seem helpless in its grip. A sad irony: millions of years to accumulate, and we burn most of it in a little less than a century, release countless millennia of accrued sunlight into the atmosphere. To what end?

Turn now. Slowly. Look again. Space. Endless space. The pale green tundra rolls away like a vast carpet toward the dark foothills. Beyond, thirty miles away, the mysterious peaks of the Brooks Range rear up into towering white and gray cumulus clouds. Have you ever seen a landscape so large, so empty, yet in another way so very full? When I look across this space, I feel a connection to something essential, the beginning of things and the end. My heart expands and I feel alive and well. Perhaps what I feel is God.

Caribou. That's why I came here the first time, to kill caribou. The fervent desires of youth. I wanted to kill all the animals Alaska had to offer. I saw no limits, no end to things. But my attitude began to change when, a couple years later, I went to work on the Trans-Alaska Pipeline. There I began to witness the destructive nature of our collective desires, to experience the price we pay to feed our illusion of technological progress. The waste, the greed spread through Alaska like wildfire. It is not a better place today because of it.

It was several years later, working in the oil fields, that turned me completely to another way of thinking. "The Slope," as it's called by the workers there, even fifteen years ago was the largest contiguous industrial development on earth, several hundred square miles (close to double that size today.) The oil companies boldly touted just how carefully they were developing the Arctic. But the reality was, and is, that petroleum production is a toxic, destructive, go-for-broke business, dedicated to one thing only: profit. The Slope tells that tale. A carefully orchestrated oil company tour won't. I've seen it. Toxic waste bubbles in settling ponds and seeps into nearby lakes. Huge holes, where billions of yards of gravel have been mined, gape like open sores on the landscape. Every turn of the horizon is broken by the works of humans: a maze of pipelines and roads, drilling platforms, radio towers, transmission lines, camp buildings, oil wells, refineries, and production facilities. There is something surreal and sinister about it, a space odyssey quality that confuses the mind, a hard, angled, technological sterility. Such a vivid contrast to this wild world where we stand today. Ultimately, though, it's the choice we're faced with.

Do we condemn this wild world? Or can we strive for a new way of living, one that honors something of both the past and the future? Do we keep turning the Arctic wilds to our own means, just to keep the petroleum flowing for a few more years, even when we know that the use of fossil fuel is ultimately killing us and the planet we live on? Dramatic words? Doom and gloom? Maybe. Maybe not. You decide.

R. GLENDON BRUNK
(B. 1945)

ENDANGERED PEOPLES

Today, people the world over anxiously follow the fate of
sea turtles, condors, black rhinos, and hundreds of other
endangered species. But we often forget—or fail to realize—
that whole peoples can be endangered, too. In our time,
as never before, distinct cultures are vanishing virtually
overnight.

More than ninety of Brazil's indigenous tribes have already disappeared. In Sarawak, the gentle, forest-dwelling
Penan have all but vanished. But it is not just at the ends
of the earth that people are struggling to survive, and survive as who they are. Right here in America, in our own back-
yard, the push for oil development in the Arctic Wildlife
Refuge threatens the Gwich'in, who depend on the caribou
much as the Plains Indians once depended upon buffalo.

The Gwich'in, the northernmost Indians in the world,
speak of their relationship to the caribou as a kind of kin-
ship. It began long ago, they say, in a time when all creatures
spoke the same language. In that distant time, the caribou
and the Gwich'in people were one. As they evolved into sepa-
rate beings, the caribou and the Gwich'in would be brothers,
always able to sense each other's thoughts and feelings.
The tundra would sustain the caribou and the caribou
would sustain the people.

Ancient memories and history flow together. Today about five thousand Gwich'in live in Alaska and Canada. In the 1980s, their cherished isolation came to an abrupt end when oil companies announced they wanted to drill for oil in the very heart of the caribou calving grounds. Fearing that the caribou would go the way of the buffalo, the Gwich'in are fighting to save both the caribou and themselves.

At a gathering of the Gwich'in bands of Arctic Village, Norma Kassi of Old Crow takes the tribe's diamond willow talking stick and speaks. "A long shadow hangs over our lives," she says. "Oil development threatens the caribou. If the caribou are threatened, then the people are threatened.

"Oil executives and government leaders don't seem to understand. They don't come into our homes and share our food. They haven't listened to the feelings in our songs and in our prayers. They have never seen the faces of our elders light up when they hear that the caribou have come back. And they haven't seen our elders weep when they think about the damage that oil rigs would cause to the caribou. Our elders have seen parts of our culture destroyed and are worried that our people may disappear forever."

For those of us in the western world who have cash paying jobs and can go to malls and supermarkets to get clothing and food, it's often hard to understand how deeply dependent the Gwich'in are on the caribou—and how reverent and protective they are of the land and its resources. Their centuries-old survival prohibition against waste has been written into contemporary Gwich'in law: One should kill a caribou only when in need and then use as many parts of the animal as possible.

Before the coming of European trappers, Gwich'in hunted caribou with arrows and spears, sometimes corralling them with carefully positioned spruce-pole fences. Today they use rifles and snowmobiles, but their traditional approach to the hunt remains unchanged. No matter how hungry the villagers may be after a long winter, they allow the first band of caribou that appears each spring to pass undisturbed.

After a successful hunt, caribou meat is distributed in the community through a network of sharing, gift giving, and trade. The meat is preserved by freezing or drying and provides about 75 percent of the protein in the Gwich'in diet. Skins are sewn into slippers, purses, winter boots, bags, and shirts. Bones are fashioned into awls, hooks, handles, and skin scrapers. And the spirit of the caribou is honored in songs, stories, and dances.

The Gwich'in still live in the spirit of their ancestors, close to the land, hunting and fishing. It is a way of life they treasure and have chosen to protect at every turn. When Congress settled the land claims of Alaska Natives, most Native Alaskans agreed to accept title to some lands and cash payment for others. Not the Gwich'in. They opted to forgo any cash in favor of retaining control over as much land as possible. Their objective was to protect the caribou—and thus their way of life.

"My grandfather built caribou fences up in the mountains and was ready to defend them with his life," says

Jonathan Soloman, resplendent in a caribou leather vest that his wife had made and adorned with beads. "I was raised by my father out on the land. It was a good way of life. My father handed it down to me and I will hand it down to my children."

I once went up the Porcupine River with Jonathan and two of his sons, 360 miles in an open skiff from Fort Yukon to Old Crow in Canada. It's as close as I've ever come to traveling back in time. The fall air was crisp and caribou were beginning to return from the Arctic coastal plain. Several bulls came to the river's edge and we took them, saving every scrap of meat, scraping the skins, roasting the heads over an open fire. We pitched our canvas tent on Caribou Bar, where Jonathan had camped nearly every fall for more than fifty years, ever since he was a boy learning the ways of the river and the weather and the caribou from his father.

All night, the river whispered along the bank. I stirred in my sleep to the sounds of splashing. I lifted the canvas flap, looked out . . . a group of bulls were crossing at night, their enormous antlers swaying like shadows over the water, and, far above, a pale curtain of northern lights hovered over the river.

We woke to the first morning of winter. The ground and every rock and tree were white with fresh snow. Before breaking camp we coaxed the coals of our campfire back to life and made a pot of strong coffee. Jonathan was quiet, thoughtful, somewhere within himself.

"Can you see how it is?" he said at length. "Can you see what we are fighting for? This is the way we live . . . on the river, with the animals. This is the way my father and my grandfather and all of our people have lived . . . for thousands of years. This is who we are. We come from the land, like the caribou. If I have to give my life to defend their calving grounds, I will.

"Why take a chance? Why risk the caribou? Why gamble with our lives? With our future?"

ART DAVIDSON
(B. 1943)

HEY MOM, WHAT DOES
REFUGE MEAN?

Yes, the caribou will have to move again.
Yes, another place, but smaller still, will have them.
Yes, their habitat diminishes in increments, but we will
    not notice.
Yes, the tundra is a habitat.
Yes, the tundra is black muck, moss, lichen, herbs, small
    flowers, dwarf shrubs.
Yes, the tundra holds a subsoil of permafrost, delicate, and
    beneath that, a long way back, oil again.
Yes, oil again. The past lives there.

Yes, even winter is fragile.
Yes, an old one will remember tundra names and shushing
    sounds of white on white.
Yes, a young one will forget its smells.
Yes, a youngster will not be taught to notice seasons
    under bones.
Yes, your own child will not ever ask these questions.
Yes, the tundra has a feeling about this again.
Yes, we still have an ancient memory.

Yes, we will deny it again.
Yes, this is familiar: a refuge unprotected.
Yes, the caribou, white bear, wolf and others without
     names will move as needed again. At least a little while
     longer. But the wild integrity will not return.

Yes, amnesia is an anesthesia.
Yes, this world will have a little more fuel, a little longer,
     again.
Yes, this is familiar: a wildlife refuge that wildness must
     flee from.
Yes, it's what we call a breach, but it's not new. Again,
     it's again.
Yes, our next patch will be less than.
Yes, there is something at stake we cannot put our finger
     on, cannot name.
Yes, it will not be the same. The sounds of progress cannot
     stand in for the wind. Things sacred but not held so
     in one time will come back scared and combustible in
     another.

Yes, we are burning the earth's memory because we are
     so cold.
Yes, we will forget this again and again and again.
Yes, this has a name.
Yes, something irrevocable is occurring again.
Yes, we will have to remember.
Yes, this will hurt.
Yes, we will have to place the memory on our tongue.

Yes, we will have to speak it in so many languages.
Yes, we will have to speak it as one word.

LAURIE KUTCHINS
(B. 1956)

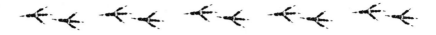

CENTURY'S THEME

Not long ago Stephen Ambrose visited Alaska as a keynote speaker in a state humanities forum, and Susan Knowles, Alaska's first lady, provided a gracious introduction. For more than an hour Dr. Ambrose, an eminent historian and the author of many best-selling books, commanded the auditorium with his raspy voice. I watched it on PBS with a cold beer in my hand. Afterward, many people asked Dr. Ambrose questions. He summarized the last century as the most brutal in human history, a time of genocide and mass destruction, but also of great accomplishment as democracy prevailed over totalitarianism around the world.

What then, somebody asked, will be the theme of the next century? The restoration of nature, Ambrose said without hesitation. It will have to be. If it is not, the earth's natural systems will be irreparably damaged and will no longer oscillate as they have for millions of years. Human beings will then have created a dangerous legacy of extinctions, toxins, pestilence, famine, global warming, and erratic weather, and every society on earth will face greater havoc and instability. The remnants of our industries, rusting in our acid rain, will make a folly of our shortsighted pursuits of oil, coal, and other economic narcotics.

A brief silence filled the auditorium. I found myself sitting stone still, the glass of beer empty.

The message from Ambrose was obvious. It was time to change. Time to come down from our throne and live in the valley and sleep on the ground. Time to cherish those things our ancestors routinely destroyed: wild places, open land, free rivers, bird songs, and wolf howls. Having reached the northern end of our continent and a new millennium, it was time to learn the meaning of "refuge" before the last one disappeared. In Arctic Alaska, where more than 95 percent of the North Slope is already available to oil drilling and profiteering, the restoration of nature would begin by leaving the last apple unpicked. Not an easy thing to do in the Last Frontier, where the illusion of wealth does not afford Copernican ways of thinking, and where the state constitution reads like a biblical edict for the subjugation of nature, and where don't-tread-on-me populists (who criticize the federal government for everything except subsidies) regard road building and pipeline laying as virtues under God.

Governor Tony Knowles thanked Dr. Ambrose for his comments and quickly changed the subject. A few months later the governor appeared on CBS's *60 Minutes* and said that drilling for oil in the Arctic National Wildlife Refuge could be done in an environmentally safe manner. How youthful and properly groomed he appeared, riding in a helicopter as he assessed the refuge through plexiglass. He came from Oklahoma and earned a Yale degree and worked on the pipeline back when every day must have seemed like payday. Now some thirty years later, with Americans driving bigger cars to and from their bigger homes, and Prudhoe Bay running dry, he said it was time to "explore" another piece of Arctic Alaska, this one in the middle of a caribou calving ground. I shook my head.

Open "An-wahr" is how these hydrocarbon people pronounce it. ANWR, the Arctic National Wildlife Refuge. They reduce our last great wild place to an acronym, perfect for a factoid culture. Is this then what becomes of our last Serengeti? Listening to them you'd think the Refuge had been closed all this time. Yet somehow I managed to get there. So did thousands of others. My first time in the Arctic Refuge I thought . . . no, wait, I didn't think. That's the point. I was so deeply touched that I walked about in a dream, as if the earth were new and dew-laden, and I was the first person on it. Or maybe the last. I watched a wolf in the midnight sun. I watched one hundred thousand caribou swim a river with ancient determination and run across the tundra with what I could only describe as exuberance. I watched a golden eagle slice the sky. I heard a silence so profound it was more of a presence than an absence. I felt cradled and deeply at home, as if all my life I had been coming back to this place. Walt Whitman once said that a man's greatest improvements come to him when he eats and sleeps with the earth. Dear God, I thought, is this why the prophets go into the wilderness? To feel a part of the first day of creation?

If anything we have moved the wrong way since Prudhoe Bay, to greater consumption and less conservation. And while my representatives in Congress say we need more domestic oil for national security, they cut deals to ship

North Slope crude to markets overseas. What then is it all about? Is the issue truly about oil, power, energy, jobs, and security, or is it about the limits of our respect for the larger-than-human world?

"Open An-wahr," they say again and again. It always has been open, gentlemen. I challenge you to leave behind your helicopters and cell phones and unctuous aides and come down from your mountain and grow a new chamber in your heart. Awaken to something that is not for sale, something older than the oldest economy. Something sacred.

KIM HEACOX
(B. 1951)

IT'S A R-E-F-U-G-E

Because the Arctic Refuge and its life-forms are unable to speak for themselves, we must do it for them. If we refuse to respect the integrity of their natural existence, we are that much less human. But if we do respect it, we are all made better, more human, even if it's just in knowing that such a special place is held inviolate for our fellow creatures— and thus for ourselves as well.

> It is only in our relations with the other-than-human that we become truly human ourselves.

Such understanding will help us to appreciate our inseparable relationship with all other species, our proper place among all forms of life within this incredibly beautiful world we jointly inhabit. We might not then behave so irresponsibly toward them and our common habitat— nor toward each other—and we might also begin to appreciate and to feel genuinely thankful for that portion of the miracle of life on earth that is given to each of us in our time. . . .

It is not energy that is in short supply. It's understanding and humility. The Arctic National Wildlife Refuge is a refuge for us too.

Charles Konigsberg

CHARLES KONIGSBERG
(B. 1924)

ARCTIC REFUGE: POLAR BEARS
AND SEISMIC TESTING

Bearing two fertilized eggs from a successful summer mating, a female polar bear leaves the Beaufort Sea ice pack in October and heads inland, onto the Arctic National Wildlife Refuge's coastal plain. Within a few miles of the shore, the bear finds a suitable snowbank, digs a tunnel into the firmly packed snow and builds a snug oval chamber. An excellent insulator, such a shelter may be sixty degrees warmer than the air outside during periods of extreme cold. This is where she'll spend the Arctic winter, when fierce blizzards can rage for days and windchill temperatures drop below -100°F. Five months, maybe more, will pass until the female leaves her den. Remarkably, she won't need to eat, drink, defecate, or urinate throughout that time. Even more extraordinary is the fact that she'll give birth during her extended fast and then nurse her cubs for several months while still in hibernation.

Polar bear cubs weigh one to one and a half pounds when born, in December or January; unable to see at birth, they have such fine hair they may appear naked. Protected from winter's severity and nursing on creamlike milk that is 46 percent fat, the cubs will grow quickly in the safety of the den and weigh twenty-five to thirty pounds when they emerge in spring. But months will pass before they're developed enough to survive the rigors of an Arctic winter outside their surrogate womb.

Now imagine that a three-dimensional seismic-testing team approaches the polar bear's den during this vulnerable time. Used in Alaska's North Slope oil exploration, such crews may employ up to one hundred people and forty vehicles, including bulldozers and huge, tracked, twenty-eight-ton "thumper trucks." Normally they operate in winter, to minimize impacts to the fragile tundra and breeding, rearing wildlife. Even when precautions are taken, such seismic testing inevitably makes for a noisy, disruptive industrial operation. If Congress opens the Arctic Refuge's coastal plain to oil exploration and development, such crews will be given access to a landscape that is known to be a core "maternity" denning area preferred by pregnant polar bears—and the threat will become real, not imagined.

In their 1987 report to Congress, federal biologists called the coastal plain "the most biologically productive part of the Arctic Refuge for wildlife . . . the center of wildlife activity." Besides its special importance to calving caribou and nesting birds, biologists emphasized the coastal plain "is frequently used by denning polar bears." It is also used, to a lesser degree, by denning grizzlies. Symbols of wilderness and raw animal power, both species command our respect when we travel through their world. But they also require vast, undeveloped landscapes to thrive; thus they are highly vulnerable to human intrusion and activities associated with industrial development.

Even in winter, seismic testing is known to harm the fragile arctic landscape. Arctic Refuge botanists report that coastal plain tundra damaged by 2-D testing in the mid-1980s still has not fully recovered. During that same period, a female polar bear thought to be pregnant abandoned her den when seismic-exploration trucks passed nearby.

Three-dimensional testing is even more intensive and disruptive than its 2-D predecessor. During the winter of 1997–98, 3-D seismic work done on a portion of Alaska's Kenai National Wildlife Refuge caused what refuge biologists called "an intense disturbance." Among its impacts: survey teams inadvertently caused three grizzlies to abandon their dens. One of them attacked and killed a worker. According to a Kenai Refuge report, ground crews could not detect bear dens until workers were close enough to provoke an attack and refuge staff concluded that 3-D exploration has a high probability of disturbing denning bears.

Based on past experiences and their knowledge of 3-D methods, some researchers warn that seismic testing would, in a similar manner, likely disrupt denning polar bears within the Arctic Refuge's coastal plain. "The problem isn't so much the noise, because snow is a great muffler. It's the associated activity, the heavy machinery and work crews," says Jack Lentfer, a retired field biologist who studied polar bears for twelve years.

Given what's known about denning bears, it's easy to predict the likely consequences if seismic crews inadvertently chase a mother and her newborn cubs from their coastal plain hideout. The cubs would almost certainly die. The question naturally arises: will this be one of the costs of doing business, if the coastal plain is opened to oil and gas development?

Bill Sherwonit

BILL SHERWONIT
(B. 1950)

POLAR BEAR PROTECTION

The undisturbed coastal plain of the Arctic National Wildlife Refuge is of great importance to polar bears because it provides specific habitat needs that are limited elsewhere—most notably denning habitat. Polar bears require the protection of a maternity winter snow den during the first four months of life. Significantly more bears den on the Arctic Refuge than on any other land area in Alaska. Approximately 14 to 21 percent of the 140 Beaufort Sea females that den each year do so on the refuge.

Polar bears have a low reproductive rate and the number of bears entering the population each year is about in balance with natural and human-related mortality. Denning bears are sensitive to disturbance and any new activity, such as oil development, that reduced cub survival would likely cause a population decline.

Oil spills from support ships, tankers, and loading facilities could harm bears that come into contact with the oil, as could ingestion of other contaminants associated with oil development. Oil and other contaminants could also harm the marine food web upon which the bears depend.

Global warming, now causing thinning of the Arctic

sea ice, could reduce the amount of pack ice suitable for denning and make protection of the Arctic Refuge and other land denning areas even more important. Protection of denning areas and use of alternative energy are much better options than oil extraction in denning areas and the resulting contribution to global warming.

There is some evidence that coastal denning, as compared to pack ice denning, has increased in recent years. Whether this is because of climate change or other causes, the importance of denning on land will increase if this trend is verified and continues.

International treaty obligations also call for protection of denning areas. The United States is party to the Agreement on the Conservation of Polar Bears, which states that the contracting parties shall take appropriate action to protect the ecosystems of which polar bears are a part, with special attention to denning and feeding sites and migration paths, and shall manage polar bears in accordance with sound conservation practices. Development in the Arctic Refuge would violate this international agreement.

The only real protective measure for denning bears is a prohibition of oil-related activity from late October through March. To concentrate all activity during the rest of the year is not acceptable, given the importance of the area for caribou migration and calving and the vulnerability of unfrozen tundra in the summer.

Based on years of personal research on polar bears, I believe that the hoped-for benefits of drilling for oil on the

Arctic National Wildlife Refuge do not justify the risk to polar bears. Their habitat deserves permanent protection.

Jack W Lentfer

JACK LENTFER
(B. 1931)

WARNINGS OF A
WILDLIFE BIOLOGIST

I have been actively involved in wildlife research and conservation in Alaska for twenty-five years. During that time,
I have worked throughout the state, studying deer, mountain goats, and brown bears in southeast Alaska and grizzly
bears and caribou on Alaska's North Slope. I first visited
the Arctic Refuge as a research biologist for the Alaska
Department of Fish and Game on July 1, 1989, when I flew
the department's DeHavilland Beaver from Fairbanks to
the coastal plain to conduct the photo census of the Porcupine Caribou Herd. For hours, we flew north across wild
country absent any sign of human presence. For the next
week, we camped under the midnight sun along the shore
of the Beaufort Sea, searching for caribou in preparation
for the photo census of the herd, then estimated at 180,000
animals. My field notes from that trip record seeing "one
group of caribou that was about 100,000 animals (photo
count was 90,000). During this flight, we observed three
wolves chasing a smaller caribou herd of about 3,000 to
5,000. The caribou moved in unison along the edges of
the herd, much like shorebirds in flight. Later, we observed
a female grizzly and two cubs in the middle of another

smaller herd. She put rushes on caribou in her immediate proximity."

This was the North American wilderness much as Lewis and Clark experienced it nearly two centuries ago—immense country with large carnivores and their prey interacting as they have for millennia. The Arctic Refuge represents a complete and functional ecosystem on a vast scale, unusual even for Alaska, and largely lost from the rest of the country.

Experiences like these, combined with my ecological training, prompted me to join over 250 other North American scientists in expressing the following concern to the president of the United States: "Based on our collective experience and understanding of the cumulative effects of oil and gas exploration and development on Alaska's North Slope, we do not believe these impacts have been adequately considered for the Arctic Refuge, and mitigation without adequate data on this complex ecosystem is unlikely."

Conserving the Arctic Refuge is not simply an issue of attempting to mitigate impacts to caribou. Safeguarding the ecological integrity of the refuge is far more complex. Despite improved drilling technology, there is the significant probability that industrial development would change the coastal plain—the biological heart of the refuge—from a wild, naturally functioning ecosystem to a human-dominated, industrial development. The consequence of such an action is clearly not compatible with the purposes for which this refuge was established.

I am not philosophically opposed to oil and gas development in Alaska. Like most other people, I also use petroleum products. However, there are some places within our nation that deserve to be permanently safeguarded for their unique ecosystem and wilderness values. The Arctic Refuge represents one of our nation's greatest opportunities for protecting a slice of wild America for future generations. I sincerely hope that the American people and their leaders in Congress have the vision and resolve to leave the Arctic National Wildlife Refuge just that, a refuge.

JOHN SCHOEN
(B. 1947)

THE CONUNDRUM OF
CARIBOU COMPLEXITY

Caribou are a symbol of the North and a species that has been central to the lives of northern people for thousands of years. The large migratory herds of caribou in North America and Siberia each have unique calving areas where pregnant females aggregate at the end of winter to calve. These areas help to minimize predation on the newborn calves, and also contain forage plants of high quality. The caribou remain in arctic tundra regions during summer, but migrate to the northern fringes of the boreal forests and taiga to winter. The annual cycles of each of the large migratory herds bridge several distinct and widely separated ecosystems. The caribou's influence on the plants and animals within these ecosystems involves transfer of nutrients between ecosystems, including their becoming prey for wolves, bears, eagles, and other predators that make up distinct populations within each ecosystem. As they die, their carcasses provide food for wolverines, arctic and red foxes, ravens, and smaller creatures that also dwell in these northern ecosystems.

The complexity that characterizes the biology and ecology of caribou includes the extreme interconnectedness that caribou have with other species and between eco-systems. We humans have been part of this network of connections, dating back at least forty thousand years, as evidenced by the dominance of caribou in the exquisite depiction of ice age mammals in the cave art of southern Europe. The close human connection with caribou has persisted to the present, through adaptations of both the caribou and the human cultures that have become depend-ent upon them. Indigenous caribou hunting cultures per-sist today within the range of all of the large migratory caribou herds across North America; indeed, their unique cultural identity and subsistence economies continue to depend upon caribou and are an intricate part of the ecol-ogy of caribou.

Comparative studies of animal populations, their habi-tats, and their ecosystem relationships have proved an effective approach in ecological research. What have we learned from comparisons between the Porcupine Caribou Herd and other herds? We know that among the large mi-gratory herds different components or factors in their environment have played dominant roles and have had greater or lesser degrees of influence on their productivity, rates of increase, and population regulation. For example, biologists in Quebec have found that the main factor limit-ing the rate of increase of the George River Herd in north-eastern Canada, currently the largest in North America, has been the relatively small extent of calving and post-calving habitats available to the herd. Constraints imposed by the calving grounds are known to be factors limiting population growth of both the George River and Porcupine herds. It is, however, the unique positioning of the calving grounds in relation to predator populations and local weather parameters that feed back on calf survival that are the mechanisms of control for the Porcupine Herd, in contrast to grazing pressure on the vegetation for the George River Herd.

The Porcupine Herd has remained relatively stable at about one hundred fifty thousand animals since its population levels have been monitored during recent decades, with slight declines in the past few years tied to low calf survival when delayed snow melt limited the pregnant cows from effectively using the traditional, or core, calving grounds. This pattern of stability has not been mirrored by herds to the west of the Porcupine Herd, the Central Arctic, Teshekpuk, and Western Arctic herds, nor by other large migratory herds across Canada. Their populations have increased, in some cases to new population highs, although several underwent wide population fluctuations in the process. It is clearly evident that the Porcupine Herd is unique in its finely tuned relationship to the diverse ecological characteristics of the rangelands that it occupies in both Alaska and adjacent Canada.

We have learned much about the responses of caribou to oil field development from observations of Central Arctic Herd caribou near Prudhoe Bay. In winter most of the herd are well south of the oil fields, but during the calving and summer insects season the caribou move through areas close to the Arctic Ocean, areas encompassed, first by the Prudhoe, then the Kuparuk, and subsequently the smaller satellite oil fields. During and following calving, female caribou and their calves tend to avoid oil field structures, roads, pipelines, and associated human activity. This is apparently an evolved behavior to avoid predation on calves. With increasing intensity of development, as new fields and systems of oil recovery were brought on-line, areas previously used for calving have been partially abandoned. Although Central Arctic females continue to calve east of the oil field complex, calving to the west has shifted southwest of the oil field complex. The terrain and vegetation in this inland calving area is less suitable than that previously used, suggesting nutritional and hence reproductive consequences for the herd.

During July and early August, when harassment by mosquitoes and parasitic flies is most intense, caribou must intensify their feeding to meet nutritional requirements. With the expansion of oil fields, Central Arctic caribou may experience additional increases in energy costs and reduced foraging time due to impaired movement to coastal insect relief areas and the return inland to preferred foraging areas when insects abate. The possible consequences are reduced body condition and lower calf production and survival. In fact, some scientists believe that the lower birth rates among adult females in the western portion of the herd, in contrast to those in the disturbance-free areas to the east, result from conflicts through encountering the intensely developed area during calving and summer.

A finely tuned ecological balance exists between the Porcupine Herd and its traditional calving grounds and summer ranges. The nature of this balance greatly limits the adaptability of the herd to the cumulative impacts expected should oil development take place on the coastal plain of the Arctic Refuge. A compounding factor in assessing impacts on caribou in any herd is the overriding complexity of changes being wrought, but yet not understood, by global climate change. It is particularly ironic, as we attempt to assess impacts of proposed oil development on caribou, that these efforts are confounded by the changing climate in the Arctic; a change attributed to the world's accelerating consumption of oil.

DAVE KLEIN
(B. 1927)

CARIBOU STORY

As I was growing up in the small village of Vashraii K'oo (now known as Arctic Village), which lies directly across from the Arctic National Wildlife Refuge border of the east fork of the Chandalar River, I never thought that our way of life would be threatened or could be lost.

I took it for granted every time we were out on the land and I was able to experience the enjoyment of eating caribou meat, watching the grandmothers tan the hides to create clothing for us to wear, learning the skills of drying meat, listening to elders as they explained the importance of our traditional teachings in my own traditional language. I thought we would always have Grandpa there to teach us the songs and dances of the caribou. I thought that our way of life would always be what it was as I was raised. I had the vision of seeing my children understand our ways, and live by them.

This vision is now a hope . . . I hope with all my heart that my children will have the caribou there for them too. I look forward to my son's first hunt and my daughter's song of the caribou. I cannot bear to think that we can lose all this in one sweep of a vote, two thousand miles away from our homelands. I hold hope, though, because

I have seen the perseverance of many strangers who also care deeply about the caribou and the *sacred* birthplace of the caribou. When I think of the thankless hours many have put in to secure protection of the Arctic Refuge, I am overwhelmed with gratitude. With so many who are on the same path as the Gwich'in following the same vision, surely we will succeed. I recall the words of the elders, "Do it in a good way and we will be successful." These words offer me strength and encouragement, even when the odds are stacked against us. My hope remains strong and intact, we will win, we have to win. The Creator, K'eegwaadhat, provided all the needs of our people, Gwich'in, throughout the generations. Surely we will live on in our traditional ways as was intended since the beginning of time. I look forward to teaching my grandchildren of the caribou, the songs, the dances, and the story of how we succeeded in protection of the sacred birthplace. To understand my feelings and these thoughts you must understand our story too. . . . The Gwich'in people live in fifteen villages in northeast Alaska and northwest Canada. We are people who rely heavily on the Porcupine Caribou Herd. We make clothing from the hides, tools from the bones, and are nutritionally reliant on the caribou. We are spiritually connected to the caribou.

> Our creation story tells of the time when there was
> only animals, the animals became people, when that
> happened the Gwich'in came from the caribou.
> There was an agreement between the two that still
> stands, the Gwich'in retain a piece of the caribou
> heart and the caribou retain a piece of the Gwich'in

heart for all time. We are like one. Whatever befalls
the caribou will befall the Gwich'in.

This is the way that we believe. Our traditional songs
and dances tell of the special relationship we have to the
caribou. How the caribou delivered the people from famine.
Just as the caribou has ensured the survival of the Gwich'in
we also must ensure the survival of the caribou.

In 1988 the Gwich'in people became aware of the threat
to our culture and way of life. The oil industry was trying
to gain access to the coastal plain of the Arctic National
Wildlife Refuge. The area known to the Gwich'in as the
birthing grounds of the caribou. In our language we call
it "Vadzaii Googii Vi Dehk'it Gwanlii," the sacred place
where life begins. From a traditional point of view as people
reliant on the land, we believe that a birthplace is sacred
and should not be disturbed in any way. We must ensure
the survival of all life-forms since our survival requires it.

Our people decided we would hold a traditional meeting, "Gwich'in Nintsyaa," to discuss this threat. During
the meeting we spoke of the importance of maintaining
our way of life for our future generations. The meeting re-
sulted in a united position of the Gwich'in people that we
could not allow oil and gas development in the birthplace
of the caribou. Even now, we maintain this position. The
Gwich'in Steering Committee board was created as the political arm of the Gwich'in Nation on this issue. The elders
delegated to the board members that their responsibilities
were to educate the public about this threat of oil and gas
development. By doing so, we would obtain support to
permanently protect the coastal plain of the Arctic National

Wildlife Refuge from oil and gas exploitation. This fight is not just a political fight, it is a spiritual fight as well. The foundation of this campaign of the Gwich'in began with prayer and ceremony. Since then, many prayers went into this struggle. We asked K'eegwaadhat (Creator) to guide our actions, and each time we were near defeat, we always overcame and the coastal plain of the 1002 area is still untouched.

These special places have to be protected and preserved to continue nurturing and bearing life. We inform the public about our belief in regard to caring for the land. We understand that we must hold the land and all life-forms in respect and teach people these values the land has taught our people.

We are asking the support of all people to help us maintain our way of life and protect this fragile ecosystem for the benefit of all our future generations.

Masi' choh shalak naii.
(Thank You, All my Relations)

FAITH GEMMILL, NEETS'AII GWICH'IN
(B. 1973)

OF CARIBOU AND CARBON

I know as much about caribou as your average resident of the northeast United States, which is to say not overly much. In my mind they are sort of like the moose, except perennially attending some vast convention. So while I am entirely in favor of them, and their babies, you will have to browse elsewhere in this volume for a lyrical account of what it is like to be immersed in a sea of them, with their great rhythmic breathing (or whatever) opening up a clear channel to God. I want to concentrate on the entirely prosaic and unlyrical question of whether or not, caribou aside, it makes sense to drill for oil in the Arctic.

In fact, let's grant, just for a moment, every possible argument to the Exxons of the world. Let's say that beneath ANWR there are vast pools of oil (though the mainstream geologists tell us otherwise). Let's say that those vast pools of oil could be sucked to the surface without damaging the environment (the testimony of every other large-scale oil project on earth to the contrary). Let's even wave our wand and say you could transport it back to the world's gas stations and power plants without it leaking from your pipeline or spilling from your ship. What then? Now is it a good idea?

Well, consider. Oil is a hydrocarbon. In the form of say, gasoline, it weighs about eight pounds a gallon. When you burn that gasoline, five pounds of carbon in the form of carbon dioxide enters the atmosphere. (Makes no difference how well tuned your engine is—CO_2 release is an inevitable byproduct of fossil fuel combustion.) The molecular structure of that CO_2 traps heat near the planet that would otherwise radiate back out to space. It warms the planet. How much does it warm the planet? The Intergovernmental Panel on Climate Change, a UN body comprising the world's climatologists, released their latest set of predictions in January in Shanghai. By century's end, they said, the world's temperature will likely have increased about five degrees Fahrenheit, with a worst-case scenario of ten or eleven degrees. That's a lot. That's hotter than it was when the dinosaurs were wandering around and keeling over and being converted into petroleum.

And so what? Well, so far we've warmed the world a degree and a half by burning fossil fuels. Nine of the ten warmest years on record occurred in the last decade. As a result, the planet is already starting to unravel. Storms are growing more frequent and more intense, and both drought and flood more common. Sea levels are starting an inexorable rise. And northward, in the area of the Arctic National Wildlife Refuge, the physics of the planet makes the warming even more dramatic. Already, Arctic ice is 40 percent thinner than it was in 1960. An area twice the size of Massachusetts melts permanently each year. Already the permafrost in many places is turning to soup. Already native peoples are reporting that it is impossible to hunt in the ways and places they have long used. Already polar bears in northern Canada are 20 percent scrawnier than just a few years ago—there's no longer enough pack ice to reliably support their long-standing hobby of hunting seals. Already the computer models are starting to issue dire hints of what happens to global ocean currents when you melt all that Arctic ice and change the salinity of the northern seas.

Already, in other words, we've gone a long ways toward wrecking ecosystems the world over, and in the far north in particular. And this damage will only get worse unless we leave that carbon in the ground, trapped down there below the surface where it can do no damage. Right now it's benign, lying in its ancient vault, but the minute it's pumped up and put in gas tanks or turbines, it turns deeply dangerous. The oil spill may not happen in ANWR, but it will definitely happen in the atmosphere. Think of the caribou as security guards trying to prevent the theft of a deadly poison.

We need to leave a lot of other carbon in the ground too, of course—in coal mines the world over, and in oil fields from the North Sea to the Niger Delta, from the Gulf of Arabia to the Gulf of Mexico. That's hard for us to hear. We've grown to like a steady supply of incredibly cheap fossil fuel. But we need to make the transition—quickly—to an entirely different way of powering our world. We need solar and wind power, we need hydrogen fuel cells, and we need them fast. We need cars that make sense (and buses and bikes) instead of Navigators and Explorers and the other military vehicles that carry us back and forth to the Shop'n'Save.

We need an all-out all-in effort—we need willpower.

And the place to start that effort is clear. It's in northern Alaska, on the last possible edge of the continent, where we can finally say no. We don't need this. It's not good for us. Eventually we're going to make this switch. Everyone knows it, even Exxon. Physics and chemistry mandate it, much as Congress and OPEC may resist. The only question is when we'll finally get around to it, and what will be left when we do. I vote for now, and I vote for caribou.

BILL McKIBBEN

(B. 1960)

JUNK: THE ENTROPY OF
IMAGINATION

The debate over oil exploration in the Arctic National
Wildlife Refuge (ANWR) needs to elevate itself above the
bogus symbology of two fanciful views. Some imagine that
we're about to sully a 19 million acre, perfectly wild, public
set-aside. Others, the oil industry and its advocates, sug-
gest that this place in the far north is too big, too remote,
or too empty to suffer effects from human incursion, or
that the technology of oil exploration is too advanced to
spoil it. For environmentalists, the challenge is to understand the complexities of worldwide energy dependence,
that no place in the world is a pristine refuge, that ANWR
is already affected by global warming and, following years
of atmospheric testing, by radiation fallout carried by
polar air currents, and that it has been occupied for eons
by indigenous people who now hold differing opinions
about its best disposition. So understanding, it is still
worthy to draw the line in such a place, preeminently
rich with life, as it is.

The oil industry needs to exercise its imagination and
draw the line somewhere, sometime. But at present, ANWR's
coastal plain, what comprises 125 miles of Alaska's 6,500

miles of coastline, nearly all of which is otherwise open to application for oil exploration (yet another problem), is not where the industry chooses to do so. President George W. Bush has claimed that "We can do both [in ANWR]—taking out energy and leaving only footprints. Critics of increased exploration and production ignore the remarkable technological advances in the last ten years that have dramatically decreased the environmental impact of oil and gas exploration." I wonder why he hasn't applied the same principle to oil consumption and production as he did to the Mexican drug trade when he recently stated—much to the relief of Mexicans—that the problem had to be addressed on the U.S. side of the border, too, where the ravenous users reside. Oil has its use problem, too. We Americans comprise well under 1 percent of the world's population, and yet we consume 25 percent of the world's fossil fuels and, as would follow logically, emit over 25 percent of the world's greenhouse gases.

Further, Bush's use of the term "footprints" is actually derived from oil industry media-speak, a language that regularly finds diminutive metaphors to soothe the public conscience. The industry refers to the concrete pads upon which massive drilling structures are mounted as "footprints." The image is not unlike one that Exxon's public relations experts came up with following the Exxon *Valdez* spill. In their wizardry, they promulgated a photograph of Marilyn Monroe's face, which, in an oddly libidinous way, was to stand for the beauty of Alaska. The famous mole to the side of her chin stood for the tiny besmirched spot—Prince William Sound.

While it is true that oil production technologies have advanced (articulated drill shafts, for example, allow for several oil pools to be struck from one pad), it is patently untrue that a production site on ANWR's coastal plain would in any way resemble a mere "footprint," or that it would be restricted to drill pads. It's not just the drill pads that are required, but also the infrastructure, something not unlike what is spread out over miles at Prudhoe Bay, which I visited one chill September a few years ago. I would speculate that there will be a runway and terminal for landing the big jets carrying cargo and workers; and the sixty-mile road connection to Prudhoe Bay; a dumping site for waste or otherwise the means to carry waste away; and the big buildings—warehousing for supplies and heavy equipment, compressor plants, dormitories, a power generating plant, a desalinization plant (providing clean water for industrial and consumption purposes), flow stations to drive the oil through a pipeline that will connect to the existing, prematurely decrepit 798-mile pipeline running down to the terminal at Valdez. The present North Slope site has all of that and more . . . 350 miles of gravel roads and a thousand miles of looping, intertwined pipe. Its 11,000 square acres are dotted with the five-foot-thick "footprints."

The better than 12,000 acres along ANWR's Coastal Plain proposed for new exploration and, one would reasonably surmise, for production, will perhaps become the same. From all this, we hope to reap what geologic surveys estimate at somewhere between 3.5 and 14 billion barrels of oil, enough to supply Americans at our current, ever-increasing rate of consumption with between seven months and a year and a half's worth of fuel.

At Prudhoe Bay, I had a guide supplied by Arco Oil to show me around. It all seemed a little unbelievable, the astonishing place I'd flown into, coming over the Brooks Range upon the vast plain. The powerful expanse between the edifices of extraction heightened the sense of remoteness and exquisite menace. It seemed to level the very brain. Impressive as it was, both the topography and the installations with their gas plumes alight back into the land as far as one could see, it was impossible not to consider the damage caused by that infrastructure . . . out there, propping up our infrastructure of greed down at home: there, the soiled wetlands, the heaps of drill tailings, the 40,000 gallons of oily waste generated each day, the gravel pits, the dumping pits, the 250 oil spills a year, seeping into the sea. The litany could go on and on. As my Prudhoe Bay guide and I sat in a GMC Suburban at the end of a spit one evening, looking out upon the gray Beaufort Sea, four Arctic foxes materialized from the ditch. I rolled down my window to see them better. "Don't get out," my guide said. "Rabies."

To me, the foxes didn't appear rabid in the least. They barked, making a sound much like a cat's meow, then edged closer to the Suburban. One at a time, they hunkered down until they lay flat on the ground, then passed their tails up alongside their bodies and covered their noses. It was a delicate, studied, and graceful motion, a long-held response to cold. I was thinking about oil, the deliquescent remains of life itself, the quintessential substance of all of the last century. At that moment, I was also thinking about the long controversy over ANWR. I remembered the words of a Native woman, a Gwich'in from Arctic Village, explaining the oil battle: "And yet it is like we are still lost somewhere, lost somewhere, that is how it seems to me."

Alongside the Suburban, the four foxes moved again, rising, edging forward, stopping, and curling their tails over their noses. I suddenly realized why they were here. This was a favorite overlook for workers. The foxes expected food to be tossed out the windows. They'd been habituated into a new dependency. They were pets. This remains mysterious to me, and troubling, as I myself feel lost. We keep bombing Iraq to protect our oil interests. We keep driving our gas guzzlers. We keep drilling and despoiling. While other choices for conservation and renewable power generation exist, we keep doing the same thing over and over. It's as if, groping in the tunnel of our own making, we're caught in an entropy of the imagination—too habituated to our ways to consider the alternatives. Meanwhile, the tunnel is collapsing all around us.

John Keeble

JOHN KEEBLE
(B. 1944)

LESSONS OF THE EXXON *VALDEZ*

Seeking approval to develop Prudhoe Bay, the oil industry assured Congress and the American public that it had the technology to operate pipelines and tankers safely. When the Exxon *Valdez* ran aground in the spring of 1989, we were shocked by images of dying birds and otters—and felt betrayed by the oil industry. Their assurances had proved to be false.

"The public, particularly in America, has been misled for many years. A myth has been perpetuated that a large oil spill is solvable. There is no magic solution or cure."

These words came not from an environmentalist, but from Dr. Ian White, director of the International Tanker Owners Pollution Federation, the industry's own nucleus of oil spill expertise. In the aftermath of the Exxon *Valdez*, Dr. White said, "The truth is that the problem is much more difficult than the media, politicians, and even parts of the industry itself are willing to acknowledge."

Now wanting to drill for oil in the Arctic Wildlife Refuge, the oil industry is offering us the same assurances, virtually word for word, that we heard thirty years ago. Then as now, we are told that they have new technologies that allow oil development without harming the environment. We would do well to remember that this is the same industry, the same pipeline, the same tankers, and the same North Slope oil that devastated Prince William Sound.

"I knew immediately this was an uncontrollable volume of oil," said Frank Iarossi, president of Exxon Shipping. "All these contingency plans, all this planning and everything did not anticipate ever having to respond to a spill this big."

Iarossi and others within the industry had known for years that they couldn't handle a spill of this magnitude. Yet, for more than thirty years that's exactly what the industry promised it could do.

As it turned out, oil skimmed from the water during the first seventy-two hours after the Exxon *Valdez* went aground was approximately 1 percent of what the industry had said it could recover in this amount of time.

"I had the world's largest checkbook," said Iarossi. "I could purchase or mobilize anything in the world that would have helped. But there was no power on earth that could recover that oil once it broke loose.

"I'd say the lesson to society is that a spill like this can happen: no matter how low the probability, the potential is still there for it to happen. Another lesson is the inadequacy of current technology. What we have is just not good enough."

As oil companies push to drill in the Arctic Refuge, we are, once again, being asked to believe they have the ability and commitment to protect Alaska's environment. Once again, we are being asked to put our trust in their promises.

If nothing else, the Exxon *Valdez* teaches us that a place as special as Prince William Sound can be ravaged by accident—and that, sooner or later, through human or mechanical error, a serious accident is going to occur. Are we willing to risk it happening in the Arctic Refuge?

ART DAVIDSON
(B. 1943)

ANOTHER COUNTRY

Refuge: 1. the state of being protected, as from danger or hardship. 2. a place that provides protection or shelter: HAVEN.

Refugee: One who flees, usually to another country, especially from invasion, oppression or persecution.

There is *another country*—beyond our need to fuel cars or computers or tanks, beyond industry, beyond "national defense," beyond politics.

There is *another country*—a place where wilderness exists unmolested.

There is *another country*—where caribou calve and nurse, where people sing and dance in honor of the caribou that keep them alive.

Another country—what some call the "Arctic National Wildlife Refuge," what those who live there call "The Sacred Place Where Life Begins."

Another country—that will be lost forever if we do not protect it from invasion.

If we turn the inhabitants of this country into refugees because we cannot control our consumption, there is no "other country" to take them in. There are no sacred places left to which they can escape.

They are the canaries in the mine of the world.

Be careful.

Our souls need *another country*.

Libby Roderick

LIBBY RODERICK
(B. 1958)

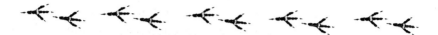

LEAVING A LEGACY

*The real wealth of the Nation lies in the resources of the
earth—soil, water, forests, minerals, and wildlife. To utilize
them for present needs while insuring their preservation for
future generations requires a delicately balanced and con-
tinuing program, based on the most extensive research. Their
administration is not properly, and cannot be, a matter of
politics.*

—RACHEL CARSON, AUGUST 1953,
LETTER TO THE *WASHINGTON POST*

The mother gray whale and baby were swimming lazily
in the water next to our panga (small, open fishing boat).
The young one was swimming over her mama's head,
nuzzling her side, even resting on her back. This affection-
ate seventeen-foot, one-ton baby was never more than a few
feet from the source of her security until Pablo, the Mexican
fisherman driving our panga, cut his outboard motor and
set us adrift in Magdalena Bay, Baja Mexico. Almost immediately the baby whale swam over to six awestruck eco-
tourists. She seemed immensely curious about this other
creature in the sea. Swimming next to our boat, she dove
as soon as an eager hand gently touched her back. Coming

up on the other side, she raised her little dark head, seeking more contact with the floating mystery of our boat.

It was this exact miracle of connection that had saved one of the gray whale's protected birthing lagoons from development one year earlier. The story is simple and worth retelling for it is relevant to the proposed drilling of oil in the Arctic National Wildlife Refuge in Alaska.

The gray whale makes a longer migration than any other Alaskan mammal. It swims nearly 12,000 miles round-trip from the cold, nutrient-rich seas off the coast of our largest state to the protected lagoons of our southern neighbor, Mexico. After a summer of fattening themselves on tiny shrimp and other invertebrates, the gray whales move southward before ice can form on northern oceans. They swim to protected bays along the Mexican Pacific coast to birth their young, breed, and rest. In 1995 one of these bays, Laguna San Ignacio, was slated to have the world's largest salt plant built on its shore: a large production factory, distillation pools, and a one-mile long pier for shipping.

The Mexican government and the Japanese corporation Mitsubishi were pursuing these plans despite opposition from local fishermen, 70 percent of Mexican citizens, a worldwide coalition of environmentalists, and millions of people in dozens of countries. The plea was to leave the area in its protected status as an International Biosphere Reserve. In February 2000, Mexican President Ernesto Zedillo agreed to visit the site. With his wife, four children, and a few government officials he boarded a panga and headed out on the blue-green water to see the whales and their calves.

Within minutes after the president's panga put out, a lone gray whale approached the boat. Centuries earlier gray whales had been nicknamed devilfish for their habit of charging and destroying whaling boats in desperate self-defense. But in the decades since 1947, when it became illegal to hunt grays, some of these creatures have begun to show curiosity about their fellow mammals and their boats. President Zedillo's wife leaned over the edge of the boat and began splashing water. The whale moved steadily to the side of the panga. Mrs. Zedillo leaned over and kissed it while the President's camera recorded the moment when the forty-five foot creature came alongside the twenty-two foot boat.

We will never know what conversations transpired between the Zedillos, but five days later at a biodiversity policy conference in Mexico City the President reversed his seemingly immutable determination to proceed with the development of the salt plant. "I have made the decision to instruct representatives of the Mexican government . . . to propose a permanent halt to the project." The extraordinary announcement marked the first time that a citizen mobilization campaign had ever stopped such a huge development in Mexico.

The 750,000 letters of protest to Mitsubishi's headquarters in Tokyo, the international boycott of their automobiles and other electronic products, the coordinated opposition of more than fifty Mexican environmental or-

ganizations, and the $10 million campaign of U.S. environ-
mental groups were all factors in the President's reversal.
But it was his direct experience with the creatures who
would be most affected by his decision that ultimately
tipped the scales in favor of preservation.

For the past six years I have been leading adventure
trips that allow people to spend time with these magnificent creatures on their wintering waters. Like President
Zedillo and his wife, I cannot fathom doing anything that
would endanger these gentle giants or the local people who
depend on the ecosystem's stability. The decision that was
made by government officials in Mexico one year ago was
for preservation. I call President Bush and U.S. government
officials to a similar courage in their management of the
Arctic National Wildlife Refuge.

Sitting south of this land in Washington state in a
house heated by propane, driving a truck fueled by gasoline, I am a citizen asking: Do we wish to be remembered
as the generation that removed the last oil from the ground
and destroyed the world's greatest stretch of arctic habitat?
Or do we wish to be remembered as the generation that
launched the nation into using its infinite sources of alternative power and implemented massive, long overdue conservation measures to preserve its greatest wilderness area?

I invite President Bush and members of Congress to
visit the Arctic National Wildlife Refuge with their families
this spring. I want them to visit local people—to eat their
food, to listen to their stories, to understand the treasure
of their way of life. And I want them to watch thousands

of baby caribou nuzzling their mothers. There is a way to leave a legacy of both provision and preservation and it is not by destroying one of the world's crown jewels.

ANN LINNEA
(B. 1949)

IN THE EYES OF A WOLF

Arctic National Wildlife Refuge, Sadlerochit Mountains.
The Beaufort Sea pack ice glows in the distance like a lu-
minous landscape painting hanging above the horizon
under low clouds, brightening the flatness of a cold, gray
August day. The tundra is changing from summer greens
to fall browns, yellows, and reds as the season races toward
winter with a hint of snow in the air. The silence is deaf-
ening in this small mountain range that runs east-west,
defining the southern edge of the Arctic coastal plain here
in northeast Alaska. Looking north across the plain, I
muse about the many times I have witnessed the wonders
of this extraordinary wild place, a land like no other I have
known.

Exploring its rivers and tundra, I have met grizzly bears,
wolves, and musk oxen, and seen all manner of birds, and
each time learned more about the meaning of this wilderness refuge. Floating down the Hulahula River, I once came
upon 40,000 head of caribou, part of the Porcupine Caribou
Herd that migrates annually from hundreds of miles away
in Canada to have its calves here on the coastal plain. It
took two days to float through the herd.

I have watched the caribou move back and forth across

the plain from the coolness of the pack ice and coastal lagoons to the windy foothills of the Brooks Range like a giant wave of life, using this place to protect themselves and their young from predators and insects. The herd uses all of this part of the refuge at one time or another each spring and summer to feed on the lush, rich vegetation that nourishes and sustains it in an annual cycle as old as time itself.

The Gwich'in Athabascan elders have taught me that this place is so sacred to them that they do not come here out of respect. They avoid impacting this birthing ground of the caribou they depend on for their subsistence way of life. They are the people of the caribou and this great herd is central to their beliefs and culture.

Suddenly, the ground begins to shake as though an animal is charging me from behind. "Grizzly!" is my first thought. As I turn to meet it, a cow caribou runs past me only fifty feet away, headed north toward the coastal plain at full speed. My second thought is what could be making the caribou run so fast? Heading back to camp, I spot a lone wolf loping toward me in the braided gravel riverbed. Following the scent of the caribou, it flushes ptarmigan from the willows along the riverbank as it comes downstream. I freeze in place and wait. The wolf is tawny with horizontal tan and black markings on its face.

Perhaps because the wind is at its back or the ptarmigan distract it, the wolf appears unaware of my presence. But it suddenly turns in surprise to face me, now only twenty-five feet away. For what seems like eternity, we look into each other's eyes. Unable to move, I feel an incredible wild force passing from the wolf to me. Nothing in my experience has prepared me for this. Face to face with this life force of wild nature itself, I feel as though all of the Arctic creatures are calling out to me at once through the hypnotic, fierce yellow-green eyes of the wolf, telling me their stories. The moment is at once exhilarating and overpowering. I am riveted in my tracks, yet unafraid.

Almost as suddenly, the wolf turns and cuts west across the tundra then circles around to the north to regain the caribou's scent, but the caribou is long gone to the safety of the coastal plain. The wolf turns back south, crosses the river, and returns toward where it came from, occasionally looking back. My heart is still in my throat as the wolf finally disappears. I begin to understand more fully why the Gwich'in do not come here. I cannot escape the fact that I have interrupted the wolf's pursuit of its prey.

Seeing that fire in the wolf's eyes has connected me to the wildness of this land with a force that is burned into my memory and will affect me the rest of my life. What I saw in the eyes of the wolf stirs a strong sense of responsibility in me to protect this wilderness home of the wolf and the caribou and all of the other wild creatures in it. I believe we will be poorer as a nation of people if we ever lose our connection to wilderness and let that fire go out. It is the life force of our wild earth, our home.

Those who witness the wild magic and mystery of this wilderness firsthand know that there is no other place like it and testify that the Arctic National Wildlife Refuge deserves to be protected and left intact for future generations to experience and behold. It deserves to exist in its own right as it is—as wilderness. It is unimaginable that this vital land could ever be developed without destroying its wild vitality. To make such a sacrifice of the best of our wild heritage for so little oil makes as much sense as burning a van Gogh to heat your home. It is a special place—a sacred place. We must let it be, forever wild and free.

ALLEN SMITH
(B. 1941)

A DECLARATION OPPOSING OIL DEVELOPMENT IN THE ARCTIC REFUGE

There must be, I feel, certain places on this planet that remain undisturbed, for what they are and what they represent in terms of a society's ultimate values. If we are to say, and demonstrate, that nothing finally is sacred, and that everything must remain open to exploitation, then it seems to me that America must relinquish all claims to a moral leadership in this world. We do not govern simply through laws and by force, but by example—by what we reveal of our basic values in relation to Nature and a resident people.

JOHN HAINES
(B. 1924)

ADOLESCENCE

The beast looming now on our horizon is a specter few in Washington seem able to measure. In the burly metaphors of war and gamesmanship, it is merely another enemy for America to defeat. And we know how to defeat an enemy. We can design and deploy smart weapons, fine-tune economies, and eradicate smallpox. We dismantled communism in eastern Europe. We will find a cure for AIDS.

In the long view, from *Australopithecus africanus*, scavenging hyena kills in southern Africa, to *Homo sapiens*, taking a six iron to a golf ball on the walled plain of Fra Mauro, such claims sound vainglorious. To put it tactlessly, the bravado is coach-talk, delivered to a team of young basketball players down by ten at the half at the state championships. In its place it is both appropriate and useful, but it is not equal to the breadth of this subject, the fate of humanity. "The fate of humanity" seems to many an overblown characterization, but only because we automatically assume we control our destiny in a crisis, that even biological problems—population growth, our essential need for fresh water and protection against solar radiation—are simply challenges, barriers through which we will engineer a breach.

It is sobering to consider in this context the quick extinction, the pull of the light cord, for *Pliopithecus vindobonensis* and ten or so other Miocene primates about 11 million years ago in what we today call eastern Europe. The still popular Victorian idea of "improvement" in the human line of descent does not apply here. These apes ceased to exist because the climate changed and they were not adaptable. Other, related creatures, including our own Miocene ancestors, were.

In distinguishing ourselves from all other animals, we have put such emphasis on the development of the brain and consciousness, we've all but lost sight of the fact that we cannot, no more than *Homo neanderthalensis* could, think our way out of every tight situation. We must face the limitations of our biology, especially the measure of its resilience in a rapidly changing environment. It makes no difference, biologically, whether we ourselves change our environment by altering greenhouse gas chemistry or, as was the case in the Miocene, tectonic activity causes climatic change. Either way the organism must prove adaptable if it is to survive.

What is unique for us as a species is that, to a degree unknown in any animal before us, our culture (behavior) will affect our potential for survival. Our behavior, which has helped create the environment we are now at pains to adapt to, will also limit, as a component of our biology, our ability to adapt. Consciousness, in other words, 40,000 years after its dazzling emergence in Aurignacian Europe, might ultimately prove maladaptive.

Many therapists have compared the rationale behind any obdurate defense of American consumerism to the elaborate strategies of denial employed by addicts. Their indictment is pointed at the rhetoric of government apologists and business promoters who, the argument goes, routinely offer self-delusional explanations (from a biological perspective) for why we can't survive without increased consumer activity, additional oil-based technologies, faster data processing, and lunar mining ventures. Faced with critical habitat issues—inadequate arable land, deforestation, the management of human and industrial waste—humanity needs these no more than an addict needs the next dose of heroin. Most everyone in government, however, is afraid to say this unequivocally; and many business people fear the economic consequences of the change that is implied.

All of us, of course, share that fear.

We are essentially addicted to petroleum. If prudence dictates we try to break the addiction before the last reserves are drained, then we have to draw a line in the dirt. It doesn't really matter where, whether it's with the high-profile reserve said to lie beneath the Arctic National Wildlife Refuge or at an obscure reserve known only to a few petroleum geologists probing the South China Sea. It matters no more than which site Gandhi chose for his initial Satyagraha, his first nonviolent act of civil disobedience.

When you draw the line, you proclaim simultaneously not one but two courses of action: reduced consumption and an alternative economics that will allow solar power and other alternatives to flourish. This story—where and when do prudent people draw the line—has become of course a threadbare scenario. The essayed intent, however, of the Bush government to prospect for petroleum in ANWR creates the circumstances for an illumination. Even while reservoirs of that other, more precious liquid, water, are draining away the world over, the biological alert still does not sound: our time is on the verge of radical rearrangement, if not eclipse. The ANWR debate is a time to clarify. If self-awareness is actually going to prove biologically adaptive, and if technologies to manufacture oil are not within sight, we need an alternative to engineering our way out of the predicament.

Is there ground between "lock it up" and "drain it" that we haven't explored? I believe there is.

In many traditional societies, perhaps as far back as *Homo erectus,* people argued when seemingly intractable problems arose. In contemporary traditional societies, it usually works like this. People (mostly people who have cared well for children) present their views and then wait, as attentively and patiently as they can, while others present theirs. After everyone has had a chance to speak, a second group, recognized by everyone present as "senior" people or elders, does something undemocratic. It makes a decision. Everyone defers to this position, however, because, in essence, elders are not distracted by the present. They speak from an overriding past, the tested wisdom that has gotten everyone to this juncture. The difference is between weather-based thinking, with its fears and options anchored in the present, and climate-based thinking. (The elders listen, first, because their decision is not predetermined. Climate reflects the measure of every weather system that moves through.)

Our deep predicament with ANWR stems from the collapse and obliteration of a coterie of senior people among us. The experts we call upon for testimony—biologists, economists, bureaucrats of various sorts, philosophers, native leaders, the elderly—almost invariably speak from the perspective of present circumstances. Testimony from a transcending perspective, if it comes, is often dismissed as impractical. With such a (deadly) arrangement, opinion, well informed or not, overrides philosophy. Senior people are put on a footing with computer modelers.

We might argue, with respect to ANWR, that elders from among the traditional occupants of the land speak for all of us. But this will not work. What is at stake is multicultural. No culture has ever been in precisely this situation. We need a "wisdom of the elders" that we must in fact make up as we go along. Given our blistering pace, of course, many believe we will be overtaken by disaster before we are able to implement any such supposed wisdom.

The decision at ANWR, it seems to me, is not whether or not to prospect for oil. It's whether someone in nominal authority—a federal president, a state governor, a secretary of the interior—will have the courage to choose to draw the line. Beyond that declaration, we require people who can think in the great stretches of time that are the natural habitat of the elders. We require a council of such men and women to restore the sense of composure that has distinguished valued human life since the advent of culture.

In the transition from *Homo erectus* to early *Homo sapiens*, it is striking to find that new tools do not turn up. The same Acheulean stone industry carries right through. But with the transition from archaic to fully modern *Homo sapiens* (perhaps due to a change in the organization of the brain among one population of *Homo sapiens* living 50,000 years ago in Africa), the most dramatic shift in the evolutionary line of *Homo* takes place. Whatever the subtle biological change, it brought with it the potential for Hammurabi's codex, the architecture of Chartres, the poetry of Blake, and the technologies of electronic processing and linkage. It is such a change in awareness as this, I believe, not a new tool, that calls to us now.

Wilderness outfitters have long known of a remarkable and haunting modern-day phenomenon. A confirmed government bureaucrat or big-business executive is introduced to a landscape undisturbed by any social or economic scheme of mankind. The response is frequently one of increasing discomfort, even bewilderment, that such places continue to go on the chopping block. It is as though they had found a lost perspective, rather than discovered an unknown one. Back in their offices, however, the recovered awareness diminishes, and it is finally extinguished before the modern insistence on expediency and conformity. What began as a profound repossession of human meaning becomes, once again, a vision for humanity narrowly defined by profit men and polls, programmers and paperbenders.

An awakening to transcendent views and a subsequent confusion about how to apply the wisdom, of course, is characteristic of adolescence. Typically, adolescents also believe adults have misconstrued the same wisdom, and that their decisions need to be questioned. Questioning the stance of the elders has worked well historically to keep human societies resilient, but only when elders have actually been present. In a culture like ours, where adolescent motivation and reasoning are necessary for the continued growth of our consumer-based economy, and where many middle-aged people resist focusing on the essential tasks of parenting and providing (beyond financial support), the trait is a disaster. More than long-term stability, what an adolescent mentality wants is to win the state championship and to win big. It perceives ethics as a necessary inconvenience, self-denial as weakness, and wisdom as an impediment to innovation. It wants biological fitness to be only a problem in engineering.

We can't afford this anymore.

What should come out of ANWR is not a debate about drilling, but adults strong enough to take an adolescent culture firmly in their grasp.

BARRY LOPEZ
(B. 1945)

THE COLOR OF CHOICE

From the *Fairbanks Daily News-Miner,* February 1, 2001:

> [Alaska Senator Frank Murkowski] searched briefly
> for a picture of ANWR in winter to counter more
> picturesque photographs used by other senators on
> the floor. Failing to quickly find the shot he sought,
> Murkowski improvised by holding up a blank white
> poster board. This, he said, is what ANWR's coastal
> plain looks like nine months out of the year.

Find some white poster board. From its blankness
scissor out the shape of the Arctic coastal plain. (Neatness
counts.) It's easier at the bottom, where policymakers drew
straight lines, right angles, gliding curves. The top—now
that's tricky, because that's where sea and ice work against
the land, where the ground is less solid, where things are
changing.

Hold this blankness in your hands. This shape represents 1.5 million acres. Go walk an acre before you return
to your map.

Open your new box of 64 crayons. Inhale deeply. That's
the smell of bright possibility. All those choices! If you
simply must have more, buy the box of 128. This is what

it means to be an American in the twenty-first century—choices.

Now choose a crayon, but first: think. Plain, dependable black, the color of oil, the tone of despair? Red, the hot hue of outrage? The seductive green of currency? The beige of compromise?

Perhaps you should scribble that blankness with numbers and words by way of charting the past and the future. Start with abbreviations that lie sodden like cardboard wafers on your tongue—1002, ANILCA, ANWR. Don't forget figures—the fluctuating cost of a gallon of gas, the anemic averages of fuel economy. Calm yourself down by naming rivers: Katakturuk. Okpilak. Niguanak. Okerokovik. Sadlerochit.

Leave room to color your map the same shade as your pickup, your minivan, your sport utility vehicle, the ones with names like "Yukon" and "Explorer" and "Pathfinder." If you don't own such a thing, surely your neighbor has one you can study. If you own more than one vehicle, make sure to leave room for all of the shiny colors.

Study your map of the coastal plain. Do you find it ugly? Turn it to the blank side. Start again. That's what being an American means—you can start all over again, try something new. Can't you?

This time, avoid harsh, obvious colors. Search your box of crayons for subtle, rich shades, or combine pigments until you can conjure the Arctic's true aspect: Musk ox brown. Meta-sedimentary gray. Bearberry crimson. Caribou cream. Hulahula blue. Oxytropis yellow. Dryas gold. Jaeger black. Grayling silver. Polar bear ivory. Lichen green. ANWR white.

Copy your map and mail it to those with failed imaginations, to those with good intentions but self-serving lives, to those who can say no to everyone but themselves.

Buy lots of postage.

Keep the original to remind yourself every day: This is how big an acre is. This is how many choices I have. This is how it feels to hold blankness in my hand.

Sherry Simpson

SHERRY SIMPSON
(B. 1959)

SHIPS ON SHOALS AND THE
WINTER OF TWO SUNS

I cast my attention northward, beyond the rain and forests of this temperate finger of Alaska where I live, and imagine the land I am asked to honor. On the way north images tumble forth, clinging to my attention like grass seeds that are hoping to hitch a ride to more fertile soil.

There is the *Princess Sophia,* stranded on a shoal north of Juneau as the last dogs of war lay down their heads in 1914, with hundred-mile-an-hour winds buffeting her frame. When the morning dawned she was gone with over three hundred souls lost to cold water that runs down the arteries of Lynn Canal.

There is Mannilaq, the shaman whom the Russians encountered in the 1700s, who would go into a trance and cast himself forward into the future. He reported seeing metal whales belching smoke as they moved upriver. He saw metal birds in the sky with humans in their bellies. And he saw a winter of two suns which made him so unspeakably sad that he refused to talk any more about the matter.

There is the memory of coming up from the sun side of a sea otter on the Kenai Peninsula. The glare of the light prevented him from seeing me until I was closer than any wild animal should tolerate. The look of pure disgust he gave me as he dove let me know I had lost his respect for using the sun in such a tawdry fashion. The wild things of this land need distance to be whole.

There is the morning I woke on Mummy Island, in Prince William Sound, after the Exxon *Valdez* oil spill, to watch the full moon roll into the never quite dark sky of summer. The stained fingers and souls of my friends who had been fighting oil with little sleep for weeks was heavy upon my heart. It was a cacophony of merry voices that lifted my sorrow. A raft of sea otters had beached and were busy announcing the continuation of life.

There is the breath of poplar around my cabin in the Wrangell St. Elias mountain range. The sweet smell of trees warmed by the long sun hours curls round my door and sings of the land as it revels in summer.

There are the Yu'pik elders guiding their young men across the tundra by tuning them to the presence of a green light in the periphery of their vision. If the light appears then they know that danger is close at hand and it is understood that the course of action is no longer correct.

I have not been to the coastal plain. But I have been with the land of Alaska long enough to know that we have the privilege and honor of living with a landscape that is still whole. The incursions of humankind are limited and have not overwhelmed the purity of the soul of this land.

A soul undisturbed is able to radiate pure essence. The landscape is the prayer of our lives here in the north.

The captain of the *Princess Sophia* refused help, betting

that the ship would free herself. By the time it was clear that the ship was foundering, the storm had become so intense that no vessels could approach. It was the last ship south that year. Some say that the heart of the northern community was broken the day the hundreds died. For here in the north communities are linked, rhizomelike, by the preciousness of humanity in the cradle of such utterly wild lands.

I cannot but see the development of the coastal plain through the eyes of the captain. Such miscalculations can have disastrous effects. In the eye of a storm it is best to honor the powers that have been released.

Lightning has been reported for the first time in anyone's memory in the Arctic. The ice shelves are retreating, threatening the walrus haul-outs and the livelihood of the small communities of the north. This winter has been a winter of little snow for most of Alaska. River guides report whole banks caving in as the permafrost of the northern lands shows signs of melting. The inland forests are dying at an alarming rate because they cannot adapt quickly enough to the shifting climate. Every glacier I personally know of is in clear retreat.

Global warming is not an argument here in Alaska. We are heating up.

Is the winter of two suns, which sent Mannilaq into such grief-stricken silence, upon us? If so, why would we turn the soul of this land over to uproot the oil and send it into the sky? Upon such miscalculations disasters are made.

There is a light in the periphery of our collective awareness. If I were a Yu'pik I might see it as green. There is a nagging sense that much is not right about the course of our actions. There is a river flowing north across the now-threatened wilderness that is still running clear and true. Listen to the sound of this water and you will know the course of action that must be taken.

DAVID LaChapelle

DAVID LA CHAPELLE
(B. 1952)

COVENANT

Twenty years old, hands trembling, throat dry, I rose to speak. It's been thirty years, but I can still picture the bored commissioner at the Alaska lands hearing in Denver as he challenged me: "Have you been to Alaska?"

His belligerence made me angry. My voice cleared. I believed what I had read in Wallace Stegner's writing, that we need not see a wilderness to know it's worth saving, that the *idea* of such a refuge creates our geography of hope.

Alaska was my icon of wild hope, a place so full of wildness and life that it formed a standard by which to measure all other wilderness. But, no, I had not been there.

Wild Alaska remains my beacon—proof that, here and there, earth still plays its symphony with full orchestra and chorus. The Arctic National Wildlife Refuge is the climax of Arctic wilds—testimony to those rare moments when we honor our covenant with our fellow creatures. When we acknowledge a sacred bond, a relationship.

The irony is overwhelming—to remain fully human and humane, we must feel beyond ourselves and live as if more than humans matters. There must be landscapes where we do not place our own comfort and profit first, where we step aside, trusting in life other than our own.

Our bargain is this: we leave the Refuge alone, we leave the Porcupine caribou to their calving, the Beaufort Sea polar bears to their denning. We protect this place. And, in turn, we lead lives less impoverished. We fall asleep knowing wildness has a shelter, and that at least one place remains where the ancestral richness of life survives.

To experience such remoteness firsthand surely would change us forever, but the trip isn't mandatory. When we need a sanctuary, a safe haven from the daily demands that grind away our joy and our strength in Pittsburgh, in Peoria, in Watts, or in West Palm Beach, we can close our eyes and picture this place.

The thunder of caribou hooves runs through our dreams, coursing like the blood of all life that we share. Wolf eyes return our gaze, we feel the tread of a polar bear on ice. We see the wildflowered sweep of the tundra and feel the sweet exhilaration of twenty-four-hour summer sun, of boundless space. Eiderdown from a nesting snow goose slips into the wind. The fierceness of musk oxen circling their young surrounds us, too.

The drum of life here goes on with or without us. The remoteness that makes this possible is the same remoteness we might use as an excuse to turn away. I am reminded of the loss of Glen Canyon, the place no one knew well enough to insist on preserving, allowing the canyon and its sandstone cathedrals to be lost under the waters of Lake Powell.

This time, we know. We know what we would lose.

And though I haven't stepped across the boundary of the Arctic National Wildlife Refuge, I have been there. I have been there journeying on the words and paintings and photographs and music of artists inspired by the Arctic wild. I have been there through the careful eyes and precise field observations of the scientists and conservationists who have studied this extravagant expression of biodiversity. I have been there, in spirit, whenever I have made pilgrimages to other wild places. I have been there, with fox and falcon, in my dreams.

STEPHEN TRIMBLE
(B. 1950)

HELL, NO. OF COURSE NOT. BUT . . .

I made a sort of vow to myself some time ago that I wouldn't support any more efforts of wilderness preservation that were unrelated to efforts to preserve economic landscapes and their human economies. One of my reasons is that I don't think we can preserve either wildness or wilderness areas if we can't preserve the economic landscapes and the people who use them.

If the survival of the Arctic National Wildlife Refuge is now in crisis, should I make an exception? Well, maybe so. Do I want that refuge to be opened to oil exploration now that the Democrats, those redoubtable nature-protectors, are out of the way? Hell, no. Of course not. I would hate to see Alaska raped by the lords of timber and energy, as large sections of my own state have been. And so I add my vote to the votes of all the others who will be saying no.

But do I think that if we no-sayers "save" the refuge from the present threat we will have saved it? I will have to vote no again, and for the same reasons that I made my vow in the first place. You can't save wilderness preserves, refuges, and parks, if at the same time you let the economic landscapes and the land-using economies go to the devil. I can't look at the crisis of the Arctic Wildlife Refuge except as the result of a radical failure of the conservation movement over the last fifty or so years: its refusal to see that conservation as we have known it is not an adequate response to an economy that is inherently wasteful and destructive; its apparent belief that nature or wildness can be preserved merely by preserving wilderness; its inability to connect wilderness conservation with soil conservation or energy conservation or any form of frugality; its cherished contempt for ranchers, farmers, loggers, and other land users.

Suppose that fifty or sixty years ago conservationists had seen fit to cherish and protect that wildness that existed on the millions of small farms and ranches that we had then. If they had done so, we would have a lot more wildness than we have now, and a lot more farmers and ranchers, and the conservationists would have a lot more friends, even in the government. And think of the wildness that still might be preserved and nurtured, and the anguish that still might be prevented, if conservationists could recognize and support such a possibility even now. Think how much petroleum might be saved if more people were eating food produced by local farmers or ranchers. If the entire food economy is entirely dependent on long-distance transport, how can we avoid drilling for oil wherever we might find it?

The Arctic Wildlife Refuge is under threat now because policy may go wrong, because of greed and ignorance in high places, because corporations have no conscience. All that is true. But a lot more is true than that. The Refuge is also under threat because we have no energy policy, no agricultural policy, and no forestry policy that is not keyed to consumption rather than conservation. Why do we not have better policies? Because there is no organized public demand.

For this, I think, conservationists must bear a generous portion of the blame. They have cared too little for landscapes that were not describable as "wilderness" or "open space." They have too thoughtlessly "benefited" from cheap food and cheap fuel. When I think of the threat to the Arctic Wildlife Refuge, I think also of conservationists and wilderness lovers who fly or drive thousands of miles to walk a few hours or days in a certified wilderness. We have got to think of something better. If we don't, the government won't.

WENDELL BERRY
(B. 1933)

ENGINES AND EMPIRE

Before using, save. Before saving, love. Before loving, look.

Today's dominion may not reach tomorrow.

A guest in a house should not remove its walls.

And who decides to burn the ark? Who defends the flame?

Even against your marble, creation echoes.

CHRISTOPHER COKINOS
(B. 1963)

ONE MODERATE'S HEART

I come from a long line of Texas earth-divers: prospectors, trappers, and explorers who have spent their lives, our lives, in the successful pursuit of oil and gas, across the miles and years. I am proud of our part in supplying the world with energy—in feeding this country—and am proud of how today's geologists have survived the volatility of the boom-and-bust markets of the past. The geologists I have known, and who are my friends, are more like hunters than farmers or gatherers, and they have kept this country fed for a long time. But because of my partnership in this family, I believe I have the authority as well as the responsibility to say no to drilling within the Arctic National Wildlife Refuge.

As a geologist, a scientist, and a citizen, and as a lover of wilderness, I need to tell you that for a thousand reasons we must not drill in the refuge.

My goal is to turn, even slightly, the heart of one moderate representative or senator—to help convince even one heart to lean further toward prudence and caution, rather than toward recklessness or arrogance, and to persuade one more vote, just one, to not venture into the refuge with drilling equipment. To not sully the definition of the word "refuge." As a Democrat, such folly would surely benefit my party, but I do not want the Democrats to gain in that manner. I want the last wild country to remain as it is, wild.

When I discuss such things with my geologist friends, they often grow combative, challenging me about whether I've ever even seen the Arctic. I have, I tell them, although I have not seen the Liberty Bell, nor the original Declaration of Independence, nor the Sistine Chapel, nor many other things whose existence and undiluted integrity is important to me. And as a scientist, I know that the Porcupine Caribou Herd might survive the exploration and drilling; though in that surviving, they will no longer be caribou, but some altered, domesticated thing, their movements and behaviors more akin to cattle.

And ten or twenty years from now, with our rising sea levels, and the soggy, warming, CO_2-releasing tundra—with our 120-degree summer days, and our vanishing groundwater, and our budget-busting dikes and levees being built frantically around our coastal cities, will any of this matter, beneath a more relentless and merciless sun, and fiercer storms, and in an entirely different world from the one we were born into? I believe that it will still matter—that it will matter more than ever. Shall I tell you once again all the old familiar stories of the oil field, or of any extractive industry? Shall I remind you yet again of our country's worst myths—call them lies, if you wish, or at best, mistakes—that the forests will never vanish and the tanker will never wreck? That the pipelines will never burst or even leak, and that our water wells will never become contaminated, and that if they do, the mining company will always, always have posted enough bond to cover the cost of the clean-up?

What greater message to send to the future than a message, for once, for God's sake, for once, of thoughtfulness and prudence, and of pushing one's self away from the trough, rather than going into the last chapel to rob or gorge upon nothing less than the spirit of that place?

Cynics tell me that there's too much money at stake, in ANWR, too much money to be made, for the "general public" to have an ice cube's chance in hell of turning this thing back, or even holding the line. But I want to believe that there are fifty-one senators who will be cautious with this immeasurable treasure: fifty-one who, even if not believing they know all the answers, or even all of the questions, will say, "No, this isn't what the people want."

I am sick to death of many of our leaders' macho swagger with regard to the manhandling of nature, and particularly our last, wildest, rankest nature. I'll agree, it's a lot harder to say no than yes. The eyes of the nation—and the unborn eyes of the future—will be watching each and every senator. Big Oil is big—I know that as well, or better, than anyone—but Big Oil can't possibly own every one of you.

I know that the extractive industries are running the show in the West, and in Alaska. Two-thirds of Montanans are against oil and gas leasing on the public lands of the Rocky Mountain Front, yet our governor and the new Secretary of Interior are intent upon drilling there. Regarding the protection of our national forests' last roadless areas, two-thirds of Idahoans commenting on the matter, and 78 percent of Montanans (and well over 70 percent of all Americans) favor such protection, yet President Bush and the Republican party are seeking to overturn that policy with tricky riders that will be immune from the public's scrutiny. I know that the ever-increasing power of corporations is leading this nation into a government led by an elite minority.

Yet I believe that the depth of the wilderness' purity is vaster and more powerful than the short-term shelf life of corporate greed. I believe deeply in the purity that lies at the heart of wilderness. I believe the vote will be close, but I believe Congress will do the brave and hard and right thing, here, rather than the soft and easy and deceptive thing. I believe that. I know I shouldn't, but I believe it. And I thank that handful of you in the middle who will make that hard choice, who will lead the way in instructing us—and the future—on how to turn away from the old patterns of profligate, reckless excess. Such a statement, and such a stand—such a choice—is far more valuable to us, and in the long run, far more compassionate, at this point in our history, than any message we have heard in a long, long time.

RICK BASS
(B. 1958)

WILDERNESS AS A SABBATH
FOR THE LAND

If you honor the Sabbath in any way, or if you respect the beliefs of those who do, then you should protect wilderness. For wilderness represents in space what the Sabbath represents in time—a limit to our dominion, a refuge from the quest for power and wealth, an acknowledgment that the earth does not belong to us.

In scriptures that have inspired Christians, Muslims, and Jews, we are told to honor the Sabbath and to keep it holy by making it a day of rest for ourselves, our servants, our animals, and the land. We are to lay down our tools on that day, cease our labors, set aside our plans, so that we may enjoy the sweetness of *being* without *doing*. On this holy day, instead of struggling to subdue the world, we are to commune with the Creator who brought the entire world into existence.

During the remainder of the week, busy imposing our will on things, we may mistake ourselves for gods. But on the Sabbath we remember that we are not the owners or rulers of this magnificent planet. Each of us receives life as a gift, and each of us depends for sustenance on the whole universe, the soil and water and sky and everything that breathes. The Sabbath is yet another gift to us, a respite from our toil, and also a gift to the earth, which needs relief from our ambitions and appetites. This is a day free from the tyranny of getting and spending, a day given over to the cultivation of spirit rather than the domination of matter.

To honor the Sabbath means to leave a portion of time unexploited, to relinquish for a spell our moneymaking, our striving, our designs. To honor wilderness means to leave a portion of space unexploited, to leave the minerals untapped, the soils unplowed, the trees uncut, and to leave unharmed the creatures that dwell there. Both wilderness and Sabbath teach us humility and restraint; they put us back in touch with the source of things. They are as close as we come, in this life, to paradise.

The Sabbath is one-seventh part of our days. Far less than one-seventh part of our land remains in wilderness. If we understand the lesson of the Sabbath, then we should leave alone every acre that has not already been stamped by our designs, and we should restore millions of acres that have been abused. We should build no more roads in the national forests. We should drain no more wetlands. We should cut no more old-growth trees. We should neither drill nor prospect in wildlife refuges, allowing those fragile places to be refuges in fact and not only in name.

Some people object that our economy will falter unless we open up these last scraps of wild land to moneymaking. They warn against the danger of "locking up" resources vital to our prosperity. But couldn't the same be said of the Sabbath? Why "lock up" a whole day of the week? Why spend time worshiping in churches, synagogues, or mosques when we could be producing goods and services? If it is really true that our economy will fail unless we devote every minute and every acre to the pursuit of profit, then our economy is already doomed. For where shall we turn after the calendar and the continent have been exhausted?

Many of the politicians and industry lobbyists who call for the exploitation of our last remaining wild places also claim to be deeply religious. What sort of religion do they follow, if it places no limits on human dominion? What sort of religion do they follow, if it makes the pursuit of profit the central goal of life? If they believe in keeping the Sabbath holy, then how can they reconcile this commandment with the drive to reduce every acre and every hour to human control?

To cherish wilderness does not mean that one must despise human works, any more than loving the Sabbath means that one must despise the rest of the week. Even if you do not accept the religious premise on which the Sabbath is based, as many people do not, then consider the wisdom embodied in the practice of restraint. Through honoring the Sabbath and honoring wilderness, we renew our contact with the mystery that precedes and surrounds and upholds our lives. The Sabbath and the wilderness remind us of what is true everywhere and at all times, but which in our arrogance we keep forgetting—that we did not make the earth, that we are guests here, that we are answerable to a reality that is deeper and older and more sacred than our own will.

For the sake of the Sabbath, for the sake of the Creation,

for the sake of our fellow creatures, for the sake of the generations that will come after us, do not violate the Arctic National Wildlife Refuge. Leave this land alone.

SCOTT RUSSELL SANDERS
(B. 1945)

WILD MERCY

The eyes of the future are looking back at us and they are praying for us to see beyond our own time. They are kneeling with clasped hands that we might act with restraint, leaving room for the life that is destined to come.

To protect what is wild is to protect what is gentle. Perhaps the wilderness we fear is the pause within our own heartbeats, the silent space that says we live only by grace. Wildness lives by this same grace.

We have it within our power to create merciful acts.

The act of restraint by the United States Congress in the name of the Arctic National Wildlife Refuge would be the most powerful act of all. Call it The Act of Wild Mercy, an interval of silence sustained in the twenty-first century.

Terry Tempest Williams

TERRY TEMPEST WILLIAMS
(B. 1955)

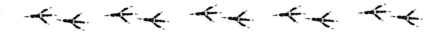

CONTRIBUTORS

RICK BASS is the author of sixteen books of fiction and non-fiction, including *Where the Sea Used to Be*, *The Brown Dog of the Yaak*, and *The Book of Yaak*. He lives with his family in northwest Montana's Yaak Valley, which, despite being one of the wildest and most biologically-diverse valleys in the lower forty-eight, still possesses not a single acre of designated wilderness.

WENDELL BERRY'S many books of poetry and prose include *The Unsettling of America*, *What are People For?*, and *Another Turn of the Crank*. His more recent *Life Is a Miracle* and *Jayber Crow* were published last year by Counterpoint Press. Wendell tends a farm in Kentucky.

R. GLENDON BRUNK went to Alaska at age twenty-three and stayed for the next twenty-five years. In Alaska he developed a homestead in the bush, worked as a log builder, a wilderness guide and outfitter, and a wildlife biologist, and in 1980 he won the World Championship of Sled Dog Racing. He is presently on the faculty of Prescott College, Prescott, Arizona, where he teaches environmental studies, and creative writing and environmental literature. Short passages from this essay are excerpted from his forthcoming book, *Yearning Wild: Explorations of the Last Frontier and Landscapes of the Heart*, to be published by Invisible Cities Press, 2001.

JIMMY CARTER, the thirty-ninth president of the United States (1977–1981), advocated and signed the Alaska National Interest Lands Conservation Act of 1980. In 1982, he became University Distinguished Professor at Emory University and founded The Carter Center, a nongovernmental organization guided by a fundamental commitment to human rights and the alleviation of human suffering. As chair of the Board of Trustees, he actively engages in the Center's worldwide efforts to prevent and resolve conflicts, enhance freedom and democracy, and improve health.

CHRISTOPHER COKINOS is the author of *Hope Is the Thing with Feathers: A Personal Chronicle of Vanished Birds* (Tarcher/Putnam, 2000; Warner Books, 2001) and lives and works in Manhattan, Kansas, with his wife, the writer Elizabeth Dodd.

ART DAVIDSON is the author of *In the Wake of the Exxon* Valdez, *Endangered Peoples,* and *Minus 148: The First Winter Ascent of Mt. McKinley.* He has been a planner director for the state of Alaska and lives with his family near Anchorage.

FAITH GEMMILL is a twenty-eight-year-old Neets'aii Gwich'in from Arctic Village, Alaska. Faith is currently working as the project coordinator of the Gwich'in Steering Committee. She is a member of the National Wildlife Federation Board of Directors, current board member of Project Underground, and a youth mentor with the International Indian Treaty Council.

JOHN HAINES spent most of two decades homesteading in Alaska. He is the author of numerous books of poetry and essays. His most recent poetry collection, *For the Century's End,* will be published by Univerisity of Washington Press, October 2001. He is poet in residence at Bucknell University for spring semester 2001.

KIM HEACOX lives in a small town in Southeast Alaska reachable only by boat or plane, population 500, counting ravens. He has two books scheduled for publication in 2001: *Caribou Crossing,* a novel about the Arctic National Wildlife Refuge (Winter Wren Books/Companion Press); and *An American Idea: Making the National Parks,* about four centuries of our changing American land ethic (National Geographic).

SARAH JAMES is a Netsaii Gwich'in Athabascan Indian from Arctic Village, Alaska. Sarah was born and raised on the land. Gwich'in is her first language. Sarah has worked tirelessly for her people as a compelling leader and spokesperson for many years. Sarah has traveled around the world to speak on behalf of the Gwich'in Nation to address the issue of oil drilling in the Arctic National Wildlife Refuge coastal plain.

DR. DAVID (DAVE) R. KLEIN, the 1999 recipient of The Wildlife Society's Aldo Leopold Award, was born in 1927. He is professor emeritus at the University of Alaska Fairbanks where he was leader of the Alaska Cooperative Wildlife Research Unit from 1962 until 1992, when he became senior scientist with the Cooperative Fish and Wildlife Research Unit until his retirement in 1997. He has done research throughout the circumpolar North on the ecology of caribou, musk oxen, and other northern ungulates and has studied the impact of industrial development on northern wildlife.

CHARLES KONIGSBERG moved to Alaska in 1968. He has taught political science at both Alaska Methodist University and the Air Force Academy. Charles has long been involved in conservation issues in Alaska.

LAURIE KUTCHINS has published two books of poetry, *Between Towns* (Texas Tech University Press) and *The Night Path* (BOA Editions), which received the Isabella Gardner Award for Poetry. Her poems have appeared in numerous publications including the *New Yorker,* the *Georgia Review, Ploughshares, Kenyon Review, Northern Lights,* and the popular anthology *Leaning into the Wind: Women Write from the Heart of the West.* She divides her year between the Shenandoah Valley in Virginia, and Wyoming's high plain.

DAVID LA CHAPELLE was raised on glaciers and other high mountain realms as a child. He draws from these early bonds with the natural world in writings about the integration of spirit and ecological awareness.

JACK LENTFER is an Alaskan wildlife biologist who has studied polar bears extensively. Jack has been a U.S. representative at international polar bear meetings, and was on the U.S. negotiating team for the International Agreement for the Conservation of Polar Bears. He has served on the U.S. Marine Mammal Commission and the Alaska Board of Game.

HANK LENTFER lives in a small house by a small stream in a small town in southeast Alaska. He spends summers with his wife, Anya, gathering the earth's gifts to fill his root cellar. He spends winters writing and eating spuds, venison, and salmon.

ANN LINNEA has been a wilderness guide for thirty-five years and is the author of *Deep Water Passage: A Spiritual Journey at Midlife* (1997 Pocketbook, Simon and Schuster) and a co-author of *Teaching Kids to Love the Earth* (1991, Pfeifer-Hamilton).

BARRY LOPEZ has lived on the McKenzie River in the Oregon Cascades since 1970. He is the recipient of the National Book Award for *Arctic Dreams* and other honors. His most recent books include a collection of short stories, *Light Action in the Carribbean,* and *About This Life,* a collection of essays.

BILL MCKIBBEN is the author of *The End Of Nature,* which was the first book for a general audience on global warming and has been translated into twenty languages. He has written six other books on environment and culture, and his work has appeared in the *New Yorker,* the *New York Review of Books, Natural History, Outside, Atlantic,* and *Harper's.* He won the 2000 Lannan Prize for nonfiction writing, and is currently a fellow at Harvard.

DEBBIE MILLER is a twenty-five-year Alaska resident who has explored the Arctic Refuge for many years with her family. She is a former teacher of Arctic Village, a small Athabaskan Indian community located on the southern boundary of the Arctic Refuge. She is the author of *Midnight Wilderness: Journeys in Alaska's Arctic National Wildlife Refuge* (Alaska Northwest Books, 2000) which describes the natural and political history of the Arctic Refuge based on fourteen years of personal explorations and wilderness adventures.

MARDY MURIE was born Margaret Elizabeth Thomas in Seattle and spent her childhood in Fairbanks, Alaska. In 1924, she was the first woman to graduate from the University of Alaska. Her marriage to Olaus Murie in 1924 began a lifetime of travel, scientific research, and involvement in conservation. Mardy is the author of several books, including *Two in the Far North.* In 1998 she was presented with the country's highest civilian honor, the Presidential Medal of Freedom for her lifetime of service to conservation. At ninety-eight, she still lives on the ranch that she and Olaus purchased in 1945 in Grand Teton National Park, Moose, Wyoming.

LIBBY RODERICK is an internationally acclaimed singer/songwriter, poet, activist, teacher and lifelong Alaskan. She is one of 225 world citizens (including the Dalai Lama, Nelson Mandela, Desmond Tutu, and Winona LaDuke) whose writing was included in a book called *Prayers for a Thousand Years: Inspiration from Leaders and Visionaries Around the World*. In addition to her concerts, she conducts workshops across the country on leadership development, eliminating racism, reclaiming our voices, environmental awareness, and other issues.

SCOTT RUSSELL SANDERS lives in the hill country of southern Indiana, in the nested watersheds of the Wapehani, Wabash, and Ohio Rivers. He teaches at Indiana University, in Bloomington, where he and his wife, Ruth, a biochemist, have reared their two children. He is the author of eighteen books including, most recently, *Hunting for Hope, The Country of Language,* and *The Force of Spirit*.

JOHN SEIBERLING served in Congress from 1970 until his retirement in 1987. As a member of the House Judiciary Committee and the Committee on Interior and Insular Affairs, he was chairman of the Subcommittee on Alaska Lands. On January 8, 2001, he was awarded the Presidential Citizens Medal. The president, in making the award, cited a number of Seiberling's achievements, but named the Alaska Lands Act as his greatest achievement.

JOHN SCHOEN grew up on an island off the Washington coast. He received his undergraduate degree in biology from Whitman

College in 1969 and his Ph.D. in Wildlife Ecology from the University of Washington in 1977. He currently serves as the senior scientist for the National Audubon Society's Alaska State Office in Anchorage. Prior to working for Audubon, John worked for the Alaska Department of Fish and Game's Division of Wildlife Conservation for twenty years. John also serves as an affiliate professor of Wildlife Biology at the University of Alaska. He currently serves on the International Conservation Union's Bear Specialist Group.

CAROLYN SERVID lives in Sitka, Alaska, where she works as codirector of the Island Institute. She is author of the essay collection *Of Landscape and Longing,* coeditor of *Book of the Tongass,* and editor of *From the Island's Edge: A Sitka Reader.*

BILL SHERWONIT has been a resident of Anchorage since 1986. He is the author of six books about Alaska and counts himself among the lucky ones who have been able to share the Arctic Refuge's wilderness with caribou, grizzlies, wolves, and other wild beings.

SHERRY SIMPSON is the author of *The Way Winter Comes,* a collection of essays about Alaska. She grew up in Juneau and lives in Fairbanks, where she teaches journalism at the University of Alaska Fairbanks.

ALLEN SMITH lives in Anchorage, Alaska, with his wife, Carol, and has been the Alaska Regional Director for the Wilderness Society since February 1989, having previously served the Society as a vice president in Washington, D.C. from 1986 to 1989. Prior to that, he served as the president and chief executive officer of Defenders of Wildlife from 1982 to 1986 and as the executive officer in the Land and Natural Resources Division of the U.S. Department of Justice from 1979 to 1982. Smith has had wide-ranging experience in Alaska conservation issues and policy since 1972. His outdoor interests include flyfishing, birding, canoeing, snowshoeing, hiking, and camping.

STEPHEN TRIMBLE worked as a park ranger in Colorado and Utah, earned a master's degree in ecology, and served as director of the Museum of Northern Arizona Press. As writer, editor, and photographer, he has published eighteen books about the West, including *The Geography of Childhood: Why Children Need Wild Places* (with Gary Nabhan), *The People: Indians of the American Southwest,* and *The Sagebrush Ocean: A Natural History of the Great Basin,* winner of the Sierra Club's Ansel Adams Award and the High Desert Museum's Chiles Award. Trimble co-compiled (with Terry Tempest Williams) a landmark effort by writers hoping to sway public policy, *Testimony: Writers of the West Speak on Behalf of Utah Wilderness.* He lives in Salt Lake City.

TERRY TEMPEST WILLIAMS is the author of a dozen books on our relationship to place. Her books include *Refuge, An Unspoken Hunger,* and most recently, *Leap.* She is the recipient of a John M. Simon Guggenheim Fellowship, a Lannan Literary Fellowship, and a member of the Rachel Carson Honor Roll. She lives in Castle Valley, Utah, with her husband, Brooke. Together, they are working with the Castle Rock Collaboration to preserve the wildlands along the Colorado River corridor.